Pascal programming: a beginner's guide to computers and programming

ISO Standard Pascal Edition

Pascal programming

A BEGINNER'S GUIDE TO COMPUTERS AND PROGRAMMING

CHRIS HAWKSLEY

Department of Computer Science, University of Keele

SECOND EDITION

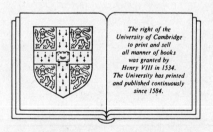

The right of the
University of Cambridge
to print and sell
all manner of books
was granted by
Henry VIII in 1534.
The University has printed
and published continuously
since 1584.

CAMBRIDGE UNIVERSITY PRESS

Cambridge

New York   New Rochelle

Melbourne   Sydney

Published by the Press Syndicate of the University of Cambridge
The Pitt Building, Trumpington Street, Cambridge CB2 1RP
32 East 57th Street, New York, NY 10022, USA
10 Stamford Road, Oakleigh, Melbourne 3166, Australia

First published 1983
Reprinted 1985
Second edition 1986
Reprinted 1988

Printed in Great Britain by the University Press, Cambridge

British Library cataloguing in publication data

Hawksley, Chris
Pascal programming: a beginner's guide to computers and
programming. – 2nd ed.
1. PASCAL (Computer program language)
I. Title
005.13'3   QA76.73.P2

Library of Congress cataloguing-in-publication data

Hawksley, Chris, 1949–
Pascal programming.

Includes index.
1. PASCAL (Computer program language)
2. Electronic digital computers – Programming.
I. Title.
QA76.73.P2H38   1986   005.13'3   86-13627

ISBN 0 521 33066 1 hard covers
ISBN 0 521 33714 3 paperback

(First edition ISBN 0 521 25302 0 hard covers
                  0 521 27292 0 paper⊦

To my parents

Contents

Preface

I was surprised to find that although there are shelves of programming texts on the market, many of which use the excellent language Pascal, none of these books was proving to be a great success with the hundreds of students taking subsidiary level computer programming courses I have taught over the last eight years. I began to ponder why this should be. Was it the standard of the text books themselves? Certainly not; several are of first-class quality with authors of recognised programming and teaching ability. Perhaps the students were not up to scratch? An easy get-out, this, but not good enough since their eventual results were on the whole normal and satisfactory. Could it be that my teaching style or ability was not good enough to support and encourage reading of a back-up text? Well, possibly, though my students tend to be a vocal lot yet they hurl no more than a fair share of verbal abuse in my direction. On the other hand, I have never found it easy to follow any of the text books closely in these courses and this gives a clue to part of the problem.

I believe that the level of background knowledge assumed in most texts is unrealistically high for a lot of students. There are two related problems. Firstly, the bias tends to be towards the numerate scientist both in the general approach and, too often, in the choice of examples. Also, the starting point of many texts is too advanced for many newcomers to computing, relying on additional course or book material to introduce some of the fundamentals of computing.

I have tried to write this book for students who are learning computer programming, probably for the first time, and probably as a subsidiary subject. It is possible that their main subject or subjects may lie in disciplines apparently far removed from computing though this is not necessarily the case. I have not assumed previous exposure to computers nor any parallel courses in computer science. The examples require only 'common-sense' mathematical ability and have been chosen from a wide range of disciplines. In addition, I hope the book will be of value to the individual reader learning to program for the first time and as a 'starter kit' for new computer science students, who should progress fairly rapidly onto the more advanced texts covering algorithms, data and programs.

I have not tried to cover absolutely all of Pascal's features in detail in order to concentrate on using the more common ones and to keep the book short. New programming facilities are introduced usually by typical examples, with passing reference to the theoretical alternatives, though I have given diagrams covering all of Pascal in an appendix. Most of the language is covered. Left out are bits of Pascal that will appeal to the programmer growing in experience who will eventually wish to peruse more advanced texts on programming and problem solving in any case. These are dealt with in chapter 14.

The text starts with a fairly gentle introduction to computers and programming leading into the basic foundations of programming in the Pascal language. The emphasis in part 2 is on practical applications of computer programming and I have tried to select examples from disciplines that may be familiar to the non-specialist student of computing: some text processing, social science applications, and analysis of collected data, for example.

It should be a source of encouragement to many readers to know that in my experience there is little, if any, correlation between the ability to become a competent programmer and the academic background of a student. A number of first class mathematics students have passed through the Computer Science Subsidiary Course at Keele. A proportional number of students from the departments of Physics, Chemistry, Biology, Geology, Psychology, Economics, Education, Geography, Sociology, Social Policy, Music, English, French, German, Russian, Latin, History, American Studies, Philosophy, Law, and Politics (my apologies for any omissions) have succeeded equally well. Yet, every year I hear 'Do you think I can make it? I am not very good at maths., you know.' Quite honestly, a positive attitude is a far more important prerequisite than an 'A' level in mathematics. Enjoy your programming.

I am indebted to many people for help and ideas in writing this book, amongst whom I must include the generations of students who have helped me to appreciate some of the common difficulties experienced by beginners. In particular, I would like to thank Professor Colin Reeves for his encouragement to write the book in the first place, Dr Neil White whose meticulous knowledge of Pascal was invaluable and Lorraine Jarvis for grappling with some of my handwriting and drawings. Any mistakes or shortcomings that remain are entirely my own responsibility.

C. Hawksley
June 1982

Preface to the second edition

In this second edition the text has been revised to conform to the definition of standard Pascal specified in the international standard ISO 7185. The main changes relate to details in the diagrams used to show the structure of Pascal but a few alterations to descriptions in the text have also been made. ISO standard Pascal has gained wide acceptance among the expanding number of Pascal systems now on the market. It is encouraging to note that Pascal itself continues to increase in popularity both in education and in real applications and that it is now available on a wide range of low-cost microcomputers.

By popular request, a set of answers to some of the exercises in Part 1 has been inserted at the end of the book.

Chris Hawksley
Keele, February 1986

Introduction

The last thing one knows in constructing a work is what to put first.
Pensées, Blaise Pascal (1623–62)

There are certain similarities between learning to program a computer and learning to play a musical instrument. In case the music profession or the reader are alarmed by this let it be added quickly that the similarities lie in aspects of the learning process and not in the activities themselves. In common with many other learning processes, such as learning to cook or to drive a car, both require an assimilation of three basic components: background knowledge, technical skill and creative art.

In learning to play a piano, for example, it is not essential to know precisely how the piano is constructed; how the hammer mechanism is made or how to tune the instrument, but a basic level of appreciation of the mechanics is most necessary. The fact that a note is struck and then decays, that the loud and soft pedals affect the note quality in particular ways are examples of this simple, but important, background knowledge. In computer programming it is not essential to know how a computer works from an electronic viewpoint, for instance, nor even in the case of larger remote-access computers is it necessary to know where the computer is located physically. On the other hand, it is important to appreciate some of the general principles on which a digital computer operates in order to gain a 'feel' for the tasks to be performed. For this reason, the first few chapters of this book aim to introduce the kind of background information that is relevant to the programming of a computer. Terms such as data, data processing and algorithm are explained and a model is used to describe the fundamental workings of the computer itself.

In the case of the student musician, technical ability must be acquired

1

through the learning of scales, finger positioning and chords, for example. The repertoire of basic skills is gained partly from instruction by tutor or text and, perhaps largely, by a 'practice makes perfect' process. The parallel skills in programming entail the learning of a programming language and the way in which its constructions may be put to practical use. Again, the educational process should include a substantial element of practical involvement: the writing of small programs to reinforce the theory. With this in mind, the later chapters of part 1 introduce fundamental constructions of the Pascal programming language together with short examples to illustrate their use. It is important for the reader to supplement this by attempting short exercises of the kind found at the ends of these chapters.

The introductory material is covered fairly quickly in part 1 and more advanced details are omitted at this stage. The objective is to move on to the creative side of programming as soon as possible, since the writing of complete programs to solve actual problems is our ultimate aim. Armed with the basic techniques, part 2 begins to explore the art of problem solving: taking a loosely defined problem, creating a precise program design and writing a complete Pascal program. In musical terms we begin to play pieces of music using our own style and interpretation.

The examples in part 2 are chosen to demonstrate reasons for selecting particular kinds of programming constructions and ways of putting them together. Thus, much of the material introduced in part 1 is revisited in the case studies of part 2 with an emphasis on practical applications. If you experience difficulty in understanding a new Pascal feature introduced in the earlier chapters, bear in mind that there is likely to be a further reference or references in the index to later case studies which may be of assistance. Also in later chapters, several new Pascal facilities are introduced which can be added to the repertoire of programming skills once the fundamentals have been firmly established.

There is no substitute for practical programming experience as a way of boosting the confidence and of improving one's ability to cope with new problems. Yet problem solving is a fascinating and rewarding art which will more than repay the initial effort to master the use of the building blocks of programming. Note, finally, that one must always beware of taking analogies too far. The fact that some musical instruments and some computers possess keyboards is perhaps the only real similarity between the two after all!

Part 1

Foundations of programming

2

Data and information

2.1 The computer as a tool

It is easy to forget that the computer is a tool constructed by man. Perhaps due to ignorance or fear of a rapidly expanding technology many people have overlooked this fact. It is currently fashionable to attribute man-like features to the computer; even to call it a superhuman brain capable of enormous mental feats performed with tireless efficiency. Indeed, this machine has become so humanised that we read regularly of computers making mistakes. Bills issued for £0.00 form a source of amusing material for the newspaper columnist. Complaints ranging from the delivery of wrong goods to the erroneous disconnection of electricity meters are put down to the apparently unavoidable occurrence of a computer error. The consequences are not always amusing. An inanimate collection of circuits has taken over from the anonymous clerk as the perfect scapegoat for administrative irresponsibility.

Yet, in the same way that we would not entertain a claim that a carpenter's chisel made a mistake or that a writer's pen spelled a word wrongly we should recognise this twentieth century example for what it is: a bad workman blaming his tools. For a computer is as much a tool as a chisel or a pen. Furthermore, it is a deterministic device. It can and will do precisely what it is told to do and only that, in common with chisels and pens. Like all artifacts the computer is prone to malfunction, but this is not at all the same as making a mistake. How often do we encounter pens which misspell as a result of the nib breaking?

Thinking of the computer as a tool in this sense provides a convenient starting point for this text. We are faced with a device which is not human, not intelligent and which we must learn to use. The appropriate term is to *program* a computer. More than with many longer established trades the technical terms associated with this tool are numerous and apt to

5

bewilder the new computer user. Where it is necessary to use these terms we shall define them at the time they are first encountered.

Having introduced the computer in this way we should not be discouraged by the fact that it is a mere tool. It is an immensely powerful and general one as we shall see. More immediately, let us examine the raw materials on which our tool is to work.

2.2   Symbols and symbolism

In computing we are concerned not with the fashioning of some physical medium as in the case of a chisel but with the manipulation of intangible symbols. Symbols have been in use considerably longer than computers. From hieroglyphics to Morse code, the Greek alphabet to shorthand the use of symbols was one of man's first steps on the road to civilisation. A few examples of symbols are shown in figure 2.1.

Interestingly, we have become so accustomed to using symbols that we take them for granted. More precisely, we do not distinguish clearly between a symbol and our interpretation of that symbol. Symbols are literally signs; marks on paper, shapes carved on stone, holes in punched cards or a character typed on a keyboard are all examples of signs. Thus, one may describe the symbol 'O' as a circle drawn on paper, no more and no less.

However, to make use of a symbol we must impose some kind of interpretation on it. Hence we may interpret the symbol 'O' as the 15th letter of the English alphabet. In this sense the symbol 'O' is an example of an item of *data* and the interpretation placed on the symbol is an example of *information* conveyed by the data. This is more than a trivial distinction.

Figure 2.1. Symbols.

CLAVDIVS IV	$\alpha\,\beta\,\gamma$	1234567890
Roman characters	Greek letters	Arabic numerals

Hieroglyphics   Chinese

Binary   Morse code   Shorthand

In particular, note that whereas the data are invariable – they are so many marks on paper, for example – the information conveyed is subject to personal interpretation and may differ widely. Thus, taken out of context the symbol 'O' may be interpreted as an Arabic numeral, the chemical symbol for oxygen, even a nought in noughts and crosses. The very personal nature of information is even more clearly illustrated in figure 2.2. The item of data 'SALLY' conveys information that is most unlikely to be exactly the same to two individuals. We may see it as a girl's name but we are just as likely to imagine someone or something we know called 'SALLY' and our reaction is coloured by this knowledge.

In the same way, if we ask a London commuter what he understands by the symbols 'PADDINGTON' we are likely to get a very different interpretation to that given by a 5-year-old child!

2.3   Information representation

Why should this distinction between data and information be of interest to us? The answer becomes apparent if we attempt to define a computer. Rather than make use of a technical definition in terms of electronics or mathematics, which would be of little use to us here, we shall use an operational definition:

A computer is a machine that is capable of processing data.

It is data which are processed, not information. Information processing is strictly for human beings. The computer can impose no interpretation of its own on data but is restricted to accepting one set of symbols at one end, to processing them in a precisely defined manner and to generating a second set of symbols at the other end. Whether or not these symbols convey information to the user is a separate issue into which the machine has no insight.

Inextricably tied up in this relationship between data and information is the matter of convention. In the case of 'SALLY' we each place our own interpretation on the data based on our real-world experience of people

Figure 2.2. 'SALLY'.

and objects. On the other hand, no reader of this text can dispute that 'SALLY' is an item of data made up of five letters of the English alphabet. That we are all agreed on this is an essential part of the process of communication which is (hopefully) going on between us. This too is information, but it is information that is made accessible to all of us by conventions that govern, in this case, the relationship between symbols and letters of the English alphabet. Similarly, though less rigidly, we use conventions to convey the meaning of words in a language. By popular consent the sky is 'blue' and we refrain from redefining this colour to mean 'yellow' or 'palpitating'.

In natural (human) language the conventions are rarely hard-and-fast. Indeed it is a common ploy in literature to bend or to break the conventions as shown in the quotation below.

> Run till you're dithery,
> Hithery
> Thithery
> Pfitts! pfitts!
> How she spits!
> Spitch! Spatch!
> Can't she scratch!
> Scritching the bark
> Of the sycamore-tree,
> . . .
> (from *Cat!* by Eleanor Farjeon)

Remarkably, we can follow such verse. Perhaps we may differ slightly in our interpretations – I am not too certain what 'scritch' means – but the overall impressions are surely communicated. Such is the immense facility with which we process language daily. But this is moving off the present point and we shall return to take a more detailed look at language in chapter 3. At the moment we should appreciate that conventions play an equally important role in computing and that we need to be made explicitly aware of these conventions.

For example, a convention which we have all taken for granted since our early schooldays informs us that the symbols

   3850

when written side by side in this manner are data that may be interpreted as a number: more precisely as the integer three thousand eight hundred and fifty. Since the computer, as just defined, is a blind processor of symbols it must be 'made aware', in some sense, of the conventions governing thousands, hundreds, tens and units. How this is achieved and whether the computer user need involve himself in implementing such conventions depends on the computer system in question but in this particular case (integer numbers) a convention will almost certainly exist. We shall examine some of the more common conventions shortly.

The above example illustrates a potential source of frustration for new programmers. We often embellish numbers with commas or spaces to improve readability. Thus the two variants

    3,850   and   3 850

are not uncommon. More often than not in computing, however, spaces and commas are used to separate numbers. Hence, 3,850 is likely to be interpreted as the two distinct numbers 3 and 850 separated by a comma. An awareness of the fact that the computer lacks our perception in these matters is a better philosophy than that seemingly believed by the student who complained that he had put the data in ten times and the computer had still not recognised his numbers!

2.4   The number crunching myth

It may come as a shock to pocket calculator fans that the representation of information in a computer is by no means limited to numbers. Indeed, it is a common misconception that the computer is a 'number crunching' device. That this arose is due mostly to historical accident, since early computers were seen as a panacea for mathematicians and scientists who needed a way of performing calculations impossible previously by hand.

For a long time the facilities available to the programmer reflected this preoccupation with numbers. Even today there are programming languages still in common usage whose philosophy of representing alphabetic characters, for example, goes something like

    let 'A' be represented by 1
    let 'B' be represented by 2
    let 'C' be represented by 3
    etc.

which makes the analysis of text look remarkably like cryptography. Fortunately, this attitude is changing and non-numerical data handling facilities have improved dramatically in some more recent languages. This is good news indeed for the non-scientific programmer. The task of formulating the solution to a problem is sufficiently demanding in itself, without having to contort that solution into a numeric code.

Looked at another way, the most primitive level of operation of the computer will most probably include instructions such as 'add' and 'subtract'. But these numerical instructions will be greatly outnumbered by instructions for reading and printing characters, for comparing characters, for moving data from place to place and so on. The computer is primarily a symbol processing machine, not a super calculator.

2.5   Data types

In an abstract sense we can imagine any number of data 'objects' representing objects in the real world. These data objects may be classified into specific categories or *types* where the data are related to their type by the relevant data convention. For example, we saw earlier how the data object '3850' is related to an actual number by means of a convention. We provide a formal framework for these ideas by considering '3850' to be an object of data type 'integer'. Thus, a data type identifies a set of values that are interrelated in some way, in this case by being a member of the set of positive and negative whole numbers (or zero). In a wider sense we could imagine data types such as those in figure 2.3. For each type, the values are interrelated in a specific way as suggested by the name of the type.

This notion of data values associated with a specific data type is fundamental to the writing of computer programs. In particular, it is the data type to which an object belongs that determines the outcome of operations performed on the data. For example, in adding two integer objects such as

$$3850 + 2165$$

we anticipate a result that is also an integer, that is, we expect the ' + ' operator to deliver the integer that is the numerical sum of the two. In another context, however, such as

'PIECE' + 'MEAL'

Figure 2.3. Data types.

('red', 'yellow', 'blue')
Data type: 'primary'

('mon', 'tues', 'wed', 'thurs', 'fri', 'sat', 'sun')
Data type: 'day of week'

(..., 1968, 1972, 1976, 1980, ...)
Data type: 'leapyear'

where, instead of integers the two values are of a data type called, say, 'string', we may wish the '+' operator to mean 'concatenate the two strings of characters within primes', delivering the result 'PIECEMEAL', rather than to imply a meaningless numerical addition. In each case it is the data types of the *operands* (the objects on either side of the operator) which determine the meaning of the operator in that context.

In practice, there are a small number of data types which are used so widely that they are predefined within a programming language (the medium in which the user writes his program). This means that the user may define and manipulate objects of these basic types assuming the relevant conventions to exist. A brief description of the most commonly available data types and their constituent values is given below. Note that this is a collection of useful, common types. An actual programming language may provide more, or less, predefined data types. Also, the names given to the data types below are subject to considerable notational variation. Commonly, for example, 'int' is used for integer and 'char' for 'character', but such vagaries need not concern us here.

Characters

The data type 'character' (often abbreviated to 'char') may be defined explicitly as a set of characters such as that in figure 2.4. In practice the set of characters making up this data type will differ from computer to computer since it is dictated by the characters that may be read into or printed out of the computer. This in turn is determined by the computer manufacturers, who have not always found it possible, or in their interests, to standardise it. Usually the differences are minor, but they can be annoying if one is transferring a program from one computer to another.

Looking at the character set in figure 2.4 we must be careful to distinguish between the characters 0–9 and any numerical notions they may conjure up. '3' may be considered every bit as much a character as 'A' or ';' or '+'. It is useful to imagine a character as corresponding to a key depression on a typewriter keyboard. '3' and ';' are keys that result in a

Figure 2.4. A character set.

space	!	"	#	$	%	&	'	(	)	*	+	,	−	.	/
0	1	2	3	4	5	6	7	8	9	:	;	<	=	>	?
@	A	B	C	D	E	F	G	H	I	J	K	L	M	N	O
P	Q	R	S	T	U	V	W	X	Y	Z	[	\	]	^	_
£	a	b	c	d	e	f	g	h	i	j	k	l	m	n	o
p	q	r	s	t	u	v	w	x	y	z	{	¦	}	~	

character being printed in just the same way as 'A'. By the same analogy, 'space' is seen to be a character corresponding to a depression of the space bar on the typewriter. The fact that the character printed is 'invisible' should not deter us from considering 'space' as a character in the same way as any other. Finally, note that this analogy can be pushed too far. Many typewriters do not have keys for '0' (zero) and '1' (one). The typist is expected to use a capital ('upper case' in computing terminology) 'O' (oh) and a small ('lower case') 'l' (el) respectively. These are four distinct characters in computing, and keyboards on computer terminals possess separate keys for these characters.

Interestingly, it would be possible to manage with no other data type than 'character' since we normally communicate with the computer by typing in characters from a keyboard and receiving results as printed characters. Groups of characters such as '123' may be given special significance and arithmetic performed by character manipulation. Indeed, this notion is reflected in the fundamental design of computers, where data entering and leaving a computer are normally viewed as streams of characters. However, to permit only characters would be particularly unwieldy and it is usual to provide a number of the other basic types described below.

Integers

The data type 'integer' embraces all positive and negative integral numbers including zero. In practice, since computers cannot cope with the infinity of numbers implied in this definition a restriction on the maximum size of an integer will be imposed. Typically, this may be of the order of plus or minus several million, but on mini- or micro-computers a much smaller range may be imposed.

Examples of integers with and without signs are

        1
        45
        −23
        +36

Further characteristics of integers will be discussed in conjunction with the next data type.

Reals

All numbers on the continuum from minus infinity to plus infinity, known to mathematicians as real numbers and including all fractions, are elements of a data type commonly referred to as real (figure 2.5). Again, in practice, a restriction will be placed on the maximum size of a real, although this may be very large, perhaps greater than 10 to the power 76 (an unimaginably large number unlikely to be put into perspective by calculating that there have been less than 10 to the power 17 seconds since the world was created).

Note, however, that despite this restriction there is still an infinite number of reals within these limits. This is because in theory there is an infinitely small difference between two adjacent real numbers. Inherent in the representation of a real number in a computer is the concept of precision, for it is impossible to represent many real numbers exactly. The rational number $\frac{2}{3}$, for example, which may be written as 0.66 recurring, has no exact representation (we cannot go on writing 6s indefinitely!). Indeed, we are obliged to use an approximation such as

$$0.66666666667$$

which may then be considered as a real expressed to a precision of 11 decimal places. Thus, in general, all real arithmetic is approximate and this may or may not be apparent to the user. The number of places of precision seems more than generous for most applications but small errors in long chains of arithmetic calculations can accumulate and become significant.

However, this is not a book on numerical analysis and the user who plans to do extensive real arithmetic will need to make a much wider study of error considerations elsewhere. The above example serves to illustrate a point which is more relevant to us here. It is not always immediately recognised that there is a fundamental difference between the data types 'real' and 'integer'. The latter is definitely not a subset of the former and, significantly, the usage of integers and reals is very different. Integers are used for enumeration: for counting, for identifying events and elements of sets of objects where the idea of a real number is nonsense.

We may take a simple example to demonstrate this difference. The length of a football pitch can vary anywhere between 100 and 120 yards. It is a real quantity, for example 110.75 yards. Even if the length is measured out

Figure 2.5. Real numbers.

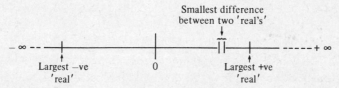

to an exact number of yards it is still a real quantity subject to a certain precision in measurement and we may care to distinguish it from an integer by including a decimal point, as in 110.0 yards. The number on the back of a player on the other hand is an integer quantity used to identify the player. We should think it very odd to see a player wearing the number 3.142 on his back.

In computers, real numbers are represented in a different way to integers and this affects the way a programmer must think of numbers. For example, it is often necessary to determine whether two values are equal. Whereas it can be guaranteed that the comparison of two values will proceed as expected if both are integers (if both have the value 2 they will be identified as equal, for example), the same is not necessarily true if they are reals. Because of the possibility of small errors in arithmetic, previous arithmetic manipulation may result in very small but important differences between the values. Hence, a value that is expected to be 2.0 may in fact be 1.9999999999, which is very close, but far enough away to deliver an unexpected result if compared with 2.0! As a general rule, it is unsafe to test for the equality of reals.

Booleans

The data type 'Boolean', often called 'Bool' or 'logical' is the simplest type of all, consisting of the two possible values 'true' and 'false'. The name is derived from Boolean algebra (originally from the mathematician George Boole) and, indeed, algebraic Boolean expressions may be constructed using this type. Apart from their role in this branch of mathematics, however, values of type 'Boolean' are useful as markers or 'flags' to denote that a specific event has, or has not, occurred in our program.

As an aside we can note that objects of type 'Boolean' are particularly easy to represent in a computer since the digital electronic components making up the computer usually work on a binary principle.

Exercises

2.1 Choose suitable names for data types to embrace the values below and add one extra element to each type.

(*a*) lion, tiger, leopard, cheetah;

(*b*) 2,3,5,7,11,13;

(*c*) 0011, 0110, 0101, 1001, 1100.

2.2 What data types would be appropriate for the following values arising in the context of a mortgage repayment calculation?

(*a*) The amount of money borrowed;

(*b*) The number of repayments;

(*c*) The mortgage interest rate;

(*d*) An indication of whether repayments are to be calculated on a monthly or annual basis;

(*e*) The initials of the borrower's name.

2.3 Study the documentation of Pascal on your computer system and find:

(*a*) The largest permitted integer (called 'maxint');

(*b*) The range and precision of real numbers;

(*c*) Whether the corresponding section of the character set is the same as that shown in figure 2.4 (part of the common American Standard Code for Information Interchange (ASCII) set).

3

Algorithms

Man is only a reed, the weakest thing in nature; but he is a thinking reed.
Pensées, Blaise Pascal.

The purpose of our tool, the computer, is to solve problems, but in order to do so a proposed solution to a problem needs to be expressed in terms that are understandable to the computer programmer and that at the same time are suitable for interpretation by the computer. A formalism for doing this is called a *programming language* and the problem solution written in that language is called a computer *program*.

Before tackling the detailed form of a programming language we need to ask what kind of problem the computer can be reasonably expected to solve and in what general terms we must present our solution. In this chapter we shall attempt to answer these key questions and to introduce the notion of a formal representation for our problem solutions. It is then a relatively small step to the constructs used in the programming language Pascal which are developed in subsequent chapters.

3.1 Problem solving

Consider the following problem:

Given the maze in figure 3.1, describe how the mouse should set about finding the cheese.

Here is a possible solution:

Solution I
1. Start at the entrance.

2. Turn left, up, right, right, down, left, forward, right, left, left, up, right, left, left, forward, left, down, right, right, up.
3. Eat cheese.

This solution takes advantage of our superior position and intellect (compared to mice). We can see over walls which, we must assume, the mouse cannot. Nevertheless, a reasonably literate mouse would have little difficulty in following the path described in solution I.

On the other hand, solution I is completely *ad hoc*. Most importantly, it does not solve the set problem since it says nothing about *how* to solve the maze nor about how the mouse may *set about finding* a path. What is written down is a description of a known path through the maze, and that is very different.

Let us try again.

Solution II
1. Start at the entrance.
2. Move forward until

   either a choice of routes is open
     or the way is blocked
     or the cheese is found.
3. If a choice of routes is open, try the right branch.
4. If the way is blocked, return to the last unexplored branch and take it.
5. If the cheese is found, eat it, otherwise repeat from step 2.

Figure 3.1. Maze.

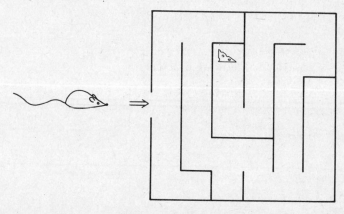

The path traced through the maze by this solution is shown in figure 3.2.

Eventually, solution II provides the mouse with a route to the cheese but it is clear that the two approaches are radically different. In contrast to solution I, which attempts to solve the problem explicitly by describing a specific path, this second technique provides a general set of rules which may be used to find a path through the maze. This is a *systematic* solution to the maze problem. For all relevant conditions that may arise in the traversal of the maze there is a system of rules specifying the actions to be taken. The decision-making process is never left to intuition, nor does it depend on previously determined knowledge of the correct path.

It is this systematic approach that is all-important in problem solving. Significantly, the set of rules making up solution II represents an abstract solution to the maze problem. The rules are not coloured by details of a specific maze and they are equally applicable to *any* maze. Indeed, it is possible that we may encounter a maze that is too difficult to solve by the first approach, perhaps by virtue of sheer size. If, however, we are endowed with an extremely fast programmable mouse or, better still, if we could simulate the mouse's activities using a computer, we may well find a solution using the second approach.

To the computer programmer, the generality of application offered by solutions of the type II above is extremely attractive. In a wider sense, the 'best' solutions to problems often embody a system of rules that solve a whole set of related problems. In complete contrast, solution I is computationally useless: by the time we have written down the instructions

Figure 3.2. Solution II to the maze problem.

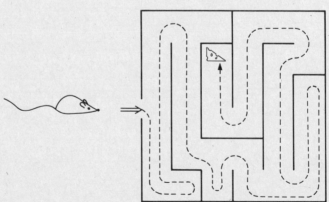

we have necessarily solved the problem manually and there is then not much point in using a computer.

3.2 Algorithms and language

A sequence of steps to solve a problem, of the form illustrated in solution II above, is called an *algorithm*. It is a way of expressing a strategy for solving the problem in a systematic manner. Thus, the creation of an algorithm may be imagined as an intermediate step in writing computer programs and we may represent this as in figure 3.3.

Introducing this intermediate step raises a most important question. How is the algorithm created, as if by magic, from the chaos of a problem?

The algorithm for the maze problem is a good example of this. It is not difficult to see, in retrospect, why this algorithm works and how it appears to solve the problem satisfactorily – it is not nearly so easy to explain how that algorithm was developed in the first place! In fact, problem solving remains an area of human activity that is not well understood and we shall return to this argument later in this chapter. The wavy line connecting the two boxes in figure 3.3 is intended to remind us that this is not a simple transformation. In general, there is no *explicit* way of deriving an algorithm for a given problem and this aspect of computing is most aptly described as the 'art' of computer programming; an art that is developed by experience in solving progressively more difficult problems.

Fortunately, this 'rabbit from the magician's hat' appearance does not mean that we can say nothing objectively about writing algorithms. Not only are there techniques that are common to many problems, and we shall investigate some of these in part 2, but there is much to be gained from a disciplined approach to the design of algorithms. We may note, for example, that the maze algorithm employs several distinct kinds of steps. Whereas, normally, the rules are obeyed one after another, from top to bottom, there is a particular construction at step 2 that obliges a conditional choice of just one alternative, and another at step 5 that implies a possible repetition of other steps. In fact, this threesome, which we may

Figure 3.3. From problem to program.

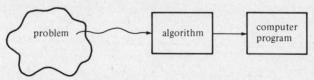

term respectively sequence, condition and repetition, forms the backbone of computer program design as we shall see later.

Developing algorithms for everyday activities can be an interesting game. Here is an algorithm for delivering milk to a house.

> *Milk delivery algorithm*
> 1. Consult milk round book (or memory) for usual order from house.
> 2. Pick up order from milk float.
> 3. Approach house.
> 4. If there is no note
>
>   then leave the order
>   else read the note and
>   if the order is the same as or less than usual
>   then leave this order
>   else leave part of order (if possible),
>   return to milk float,
>   pick up the rest and take it to the house.
> 5. If there are empties, pick them up.
> 6. Return to milk float and store any empties.
> 7. Mark any changes to the order in the milk round book.

Clearly, this is not a very good algorithm – it is doubtful whether many people would get their milk in time for breakfast if milkmen did not anticipate changes in orders and, in practice, they will deal with a group of houses together. However, to attempt to incorporate rules such as 'if the sun is shining then Mr Jones is likely to want an extra pint today' would only invite further suggestions for inclusion. We are not seriously trying to describe the activity in any sense of completeness and, in common with many everyday activities requiring intuition, an exhaustive algorithm probably does not exist. Here, the algorithm is extremely informal.

In fact, the difference between an algorithm and a computer program is precisely this matter of the formality of language. Both of the algorithms we have met have been written in an abbreviated form of English, a natural language. Although they may look quite explicit in their meanings this is only because we have at our fingertips a remarkable wealth of knowledge about the use of our language and about the environment of the problem itself. In the milk delivery algorithm, for example, we make no attempt to define what a 'milk float' or 'empties' are, nor what to 'consult' a milk round book means. We take in our stride the reference to 'the last unexplored branch' and the interpretation of 'the way is blocked' in the maze algorithm. It is only when we stop for a moment to think more closely about this 'reading between the lines' that we begin to appreciate the complexity of the underlying processing performed by humans with great facility.

The deterministic computer does not share this ingrained experience of the real world. The set of instructions obeyed by a computer makes up an artificial language that does not leave room for the subtleties of natural language. Each instruction to be obeyed has an unambiguous well-defined interpretation in the context in which it occurs and the computer programmer must learn to express algorithms within these constraints.

Having introduced the notion of language there are two linguistic terms that are carried over into computing from natural language study. That part of the grammar of a language that concerns the *structure* of words and phrases is called *syntax*. Matters relating to the *meaning* of these words and phrases are covered by the term *semantics*. Hence, for example, the phrase 'The girl what is pretty' is syntactically incorrect according to the grammatical rules of English. On the other hand, the sentence (proposed by the linguist Noam Chomsky) 'Colourless green ideas sleep furiously' is semantic nonsense (although it could be argued that it is syntactically correct!). We shall see that this distinction between syntax and semantics plays an important role in computer programming.

Note that the difference between an artificial language in which we write programs and a natural language such as English is more than syntactic complexity. Certainly, English has a very complex syntax but, in addition, there are countless examples of where a sentence cannot be unambiguously analysed by syntax alone: an unacceptable condition in a programming language. Sometimes this is due to word sense ambiguity, as in the two interpretations of 'foot' in the command 'move one foot forward'. As an aside, it is worth noting that it was a misunderstanding of the importance of the role played by semantic and extra-linguistic knowledge that frustrated massive efforts during the 1950s and early 1960s to translate from one natural language into another by computer. It is not difficult to see, in retrospect, that it was quite reasonable for a translation program based largely on syntax to translate the English source text 'out of sight, out of mind' into the Russian language equivalent of 'invisible imbecile'. Some more grammatical examples are mentioned in chapter 12.

The above examples illustrate that English is not a good medium for communicating with computers. Existing programming languages avoid the problems referred to by adhering to a relatively limited syntax which may be parsed automatically and unambiguously. Parsing is the activity concerned with analysing a statement in a language into its constituent syntactic components and this term is also carried over into programming languages. However, the fact that a programming language does not allow us the syntactic freedom of English is not in itself a disadvantage. Whilst it is convenient in the early stages to use an abbreviated form of English to describe a proposed solution to a problem, the more formal constraints of a programming language play a positive role in crystallising that description. Looked at another way, if we are unable to express the solution to a problem in a relatively simple formal language this probably means we do not fully understand that problem. We should not expect the computer to offer greater insight.

3.3   Another myth

Is there a limit to the problems computers can solve?

To conclude this chapter on algorithms it is worth devoting brief attention to some limitations of computers and their problem solving capabilities. This is not a matter of purely academic interest since it has a bearing on a number of popular conceptions of the future potential of computers. We hear fears expressed that it is only a matter of time before computers 'take over the world', with implications that we mere mortals will be reduced to slaves of some new, greater intelligence. While this is an extreme viewpoint, in general the limitations of computer applications are not well-understood by the general public. Can we draw any conclusions about such potential applications in the light of our discussion on problem solving?

It was mentioned earlier that there are no general rules to formulate an algorithm for a given problem. There is a close parallel here with that important aspect of scientific inquiry: the derivation of scientific theories from empirical data. It has been suggested that, in general, we are quite unable to derive scientific theories automatically from observed evidence. This notion is bluntly expressed in the following quotation:

> There are, then, no generally applicable 'rules of induction' by which hypotheses or theories can be mechanically derived or inferred from empirical data. The transition from data to theory requires creative imagination. Scientific hypotheses and theories are not *derived* from observed facts, but *invented* in order to account for them. They constitute guesses at the connections that

might obtain between the phenomena under study, at uniformities and patterns that might underlie their occurrence. 'Happy guesses' of this kind require great ingenuity,...
Philosophy of Natural Science, Carl G. Hempel (Prentice Hall, Englewood Cliffs, 1966, p. 15).

In a similar way, we seem unable to generate algorithms inductively from the observed data and expected results of a general problem. Perhaps more poignantly, in general the computer itself cannot devise algorithms. The computer can do only what it is told to do and if we cannot tell ourselves how we solve problems we cannot tell the computer either!

By implication, the role that cannot be usurped by our deterministic computer is that of making the ingenious 'happy guesses' on the way to devising an algorithm. Indeed, our own 'happy guesses' are often not yet good enough to provide the computer with satisfactory algorithms and this explains the inadequacy of our current 'natural-language-understanding' programs, or the impossibility of instructing the computer to find a cure for the common cold. Moreover, it can be proved that no algorithms can be written to solve certain problems.

At a more down to earth level it is interesting to note that computer programming is not a skill that is acquired primarily by the study of advanced mathematics or science as is often suggested. Certainly, problem solving requires a disciplined approach and the exposure to systematic techniques experienced by the scientist is valuable. Yet equally valuable experience is to be encountered in many other disciplines; for example, in musical transposition, in the grammatical analysis of natural language and in social science experimentation.

As a final comment, it is more fruitful to consider that the roles of man and machine in the problem solving process are complementary rather than competitive. Whereas the computer has been engineered superbly for executing algorithms, the human brain was engineered (with unimpeachable quality of design) for quite different processes.

Exercises

3.1 Modify the algorithm for the maze solution in figure 3.2 so that the first action on encountering a choice of routes is to take the *left* branch and then trace the route through the maze.

3.2 Mark likely syntactic and semantic errors in the following statements:

(*a*) The data is in the computer.

(*b*) The computer ate the banana.

How many potential (if odd!) interpretations of the sentence 'Time flies like an arrow' can you identify?

3.3 Write an informal algorithm for one of the following:

(*a*) Making a cup of coffee.

(*b*) Getting dressed.

(*c*) Taking a car out of a garage.

Computers and programs

The technology behind the computer has advanced quite dramatically over the last thirty years. Early valve computers gave way to transistors, transistors to integrated circuits and, more recently, the microprocessor, the 'computer on a chip' has appeared. The age of the personal computer is upon us before many of the big sixties mainframe computers have reached the scrap heap.

Amid this technological revolution it is perhaps surprising to realise that the fundamental computer programming principles defined by Dr Von Neuman over thirty years ago remain substantially unaltered. Computers have become faster, smaller in physical size and larger in capacity but the way in which they operate from a programmer's point of view is little changed.

In this chapter we shall study some of these computer programming characteristics and hence discover in more concrete terms how our tool, the computer, may be put to work. Two different aspects of a computer system become apparent here. The *hardware* consists of the tangible pieces of the computer – the electronic circuits, the magnetic tapes, keyboards and displays etc. The intangible programs which enable the computer to perform useful work are referred to by the term *software* and it is on the software that we shall be concentrating later. Firstly, however, a brief overview of the component parts of a computer system will assist us in appreciating the vehicle on which software may be developed.

4.1 A computer model

There are many angles from which to view a computer system. One could start from a hardware viewpoint and introduce elements of digital electronics into the description. Another approach might begin by describing items of equipment used in computing such as a card reader or a line printer. However, we are less interested for the moment in the mechanisms used to construct computing devices than we are in the logical operation of, and relationships between, the basic components. For this latter point of view we consider a 'black-box' model shown in figure 4.1 and in the discussion that follows it is largely irrelevant what physical mechanisms the boxes contain. Thus, they may well contain electronic circuits but the same external effect may be achieved, perhaps, using a steam engine with pistons and valves or even by a person equipped with pencil and paper.

At the heart of the computer lies the *central processing unit* (CPU for short). This is made up of a *control unit*, whose task is to direct the execution of a program, and an *arithmetic unit* to perform basic operations such as adding, subtracting or comparing items of data. There is also a *store*, in which a program and its data are retained and from which data are communicated to the CPU. Again under the control of the CPU, data may be moved into, and out of, the store via *input* and *output* devices respectively.

The store consists of a series of storage locations, each identified by an address, in which we may keep program instructions and items of data. We may compare the store to a rack of pigeon holes used to hold mail: the store contents correspond to the mail in the rack whilst the address of the location is analogous to the name above the pigeon hole. In the same way that mail may be removed or replaced in the pigeon holes so the contents of a store location may be changed. A typical computer will

Figure 4.1. A 'black-box' computer.

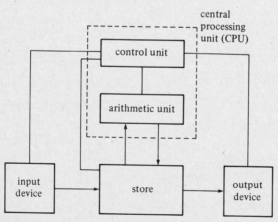

contain thousands, perhaps hundreds of thousands of such storage locations.

One of the characteristics of a computer, separating it from a simple calculator, for example, is the notion of a *stored program*. In its most basic form, a calculator is operated by keying in a number, depressing an operator key (+, for example), keying in a second number and pressing the equals button to obtain the result. Thus, the instructions to perform chains of operations are not stored within the device but are executed immediately they are entered by the user. In a computer, all instructions (the program) are entered into the store *before* they are obeyed. On a command to begin, instructions are taken from the store in sequence and executed one by one by the control unit.

Careful distinction must be drawn here between the program instructions, which specify the action to be taken, and the program data on which those instructions operate. We may illustrate this by an example. Suppose the task of the computer is to read in three integers, to add them together and print out the result. We may express this task algorithmically:

```
read 1st number
read 2nd number
read 3rd number
add numbers
print the sum.
```

As discussed earlier, the informal nature of the language in which this problem is formulated does not lend itself to being easily interpreted by a computer. The same task is written below in the programming language Pascal.

```
read(a);
read(b);
read(c);
sum: = a+b+c;
write(sum)
```

In this program, the ambiguity associated with the terms '1st number', '2nd number' etc. referred to in the former description is eliminated by use of the symbolic entities 'a', 'b', etc. However, putting aside detailed examination of the statements in this program to later chapters, let us examine the way in which a computer would obey such a program in the terms of our black-box model.

With any program the first step is to convert the statements into a basic machine representation and to store the set of instructions making up this representation in the computer store. Conceptually, we shall divide the store into two, one side to hold the program and the other the data, in order to emphasise the difference, as shown in figure 4.2. (In practice, the same physical store may be used for either purpose.) In figure 4.2 the program is shown in its original form rather than in a basic machine representation which would be too obscure and difficult to follow. The explanation that follows, however, is unchanged by this simplification.

Before the program can be executed we need four storage locations in which to hold the data for this program. These are reserved for the quantities 'a', 'b', 'c' and 'sum' and we shall assume that each is just the right size and shape to hold an integer. Since such a location is capable of holding *any* integer we refer to 'a', 'b', 'c' etc. as *variables*. (More technically, we shall call the computer analogue of the name over the pigeon-hole the *identifier* of that location.)

The program is now stored in the computer ready to be obeyed, instruction by instruction from top to bottom. Note that up to this point there has been no mention of any actual numbers to be added together, merely a detailed formal description of how to do the addition. Not until the program is obeyed do we provide the numbers and this is fundamental to programming – we write the program in abstract terms and provide the specific input data at execution or *run-time*, that is, when the program is obeyed. The action of obeying the first three statements is to fetch numbers presented to the input device and to copy their values into the data locations specified ('a', 'b' and 'c') as shown in figure 4.3.

Obeying the instruction 'sum: = a + b + c' involves use of the arithmetic unit to perform the addition, with the result being placed in the location identified by 'sum'. A copy of the sum is transferred to an output device, and hence to the outside world, by the 'write' statement.

Figure 4.2. A stored program.

	a	b

read(a);
read(b);
read(c);
	c	sum

sum:= a + b + c; write(sum)		
STORE		
PROGRAM	DATA	

Note finally in this example that the same program may be re-run as many times as desired to find the sums of *any* three integers.

4.2   Programming languages

It was assumed in working through the last example that the black-box computer obeyed directly such instructions as 'read' and 'write'. In practice, it is most unlikely that the hardware of the computer system will be capable of accepting directly such complex instructions as these (though this is not inconceivable in the future). The primitive level of operation of the computer consists of very basic instructions written in the *machine code* of that particular machine, with different machines using different codes. Programs in machine code may be made up of strings of binary digits – 0s and 1s – which are decoded by the computer hardware.

By careful study of a computer manufacturer's documentation it is possible to write programs directly in machine code. However, the investment in time and effort to do so is substantial and the size of problem that could be tackled is severely limited. Historically, the first developments in the area of a language more suitable for programming resulted in the arrival of Assembly languages. In essence, these are usually little more advanced than machine code but they enable programs to be written in a symbolic representation in place of the binary code. The generic term for all languages of this nature, which reflect the basic machine architecture, is 'low-level' or 'machine-oriented'.

Programming in a low-level language suffers from some serious drawbacks. Such languages are often quite difficult to learn and to use; it is easy to make mistakes and often difficult to find them and programs cannot be transferred to a computer with a different machine code. Perhaps more importantly, the task of programming in a low-level language is demanding

Figure 4.3. Data values for a, b and c.

		a	b

	read(a);
	read(b);
	read(c);
	sum:=a + b + c;
	write(sum)
		23	17

→6 →17 →23——→ From input device		c	sum
		6	

in itself, diverting attention away from the particular problem one is trying to solve. It is only to be recommended in a few cases where efficiency in program execution or detailed control of certain specific machine features cannot yet be achieved by other means.

The alternative approach is to write programs in a more sophisticated 'high-level' language which may be converted subsequently into machine code. Such languages are also called 'problem-oriented' languages since they are designed to provide facilities that are more suitable for problem solving. In this sense we may imagine a program written in a high-level language as an intermediate step between an algorithm, written in an abbreviated form of English, perhaps, and a machine-code program, as shown in figure 4.4.

The key to being able to program a computer at this high level is to design a language that is convenient to use *and* which may be translated unambiguously and *automatically* into the basic machine code of the computer. By restricting the grammar of a high-level language to an unambiguous well-defined syntax we may use a specially written program called a *compiler* to perform the translation automatically, thus generating a program in the machine code of the computer being used. The instructions used in the 'black-box program' are examples of statements in a high-level language.

The benefits of high-level language programming are substantial. The programmer is relieved of the necessity to understand the intricacies of the machine code of the computer and may concentrate on solving the problem in hand. Careful design of the language and its compiler can provide superior error diagnosis in terms that are easier for the programmer to understand. Indeed, it is often convenient to imagine that the low-level aspect of the computer does not even exist; that the computer obeys high-level language statements in a manner similar to our black-box model. It is the freedom to do this that is largely responsible for extending the problem-solving capabilities of computers to a much wider population.

The high-level language *Pascal* is chosen for this text. Pascal was designed with the dual aims of providing a programming language that has both well-structured programming facilities for the user and that may be compiled into machine code particularly efficiently. There are many

Figure 4.4. High-level language.

other languages in common usage, some good and some not so good from a programmer's viewpoint, but the continued growth in popularity of Pascal, including a considerable expansion in usage in programming small mini- and micro-computers is particularly encouraging. Most importantly, Pascal embodies many of the features that are widely acclaimed today as being vital to good programming practice.

4.3 Operating systems

Writing programs in high-level languages requires quite extensive support from a computer system. As well as a compiler to translate the program into a machine-oriented language, software is also needed to enable programs to be entered into the computer in the first place, to edit mistakes and, perhaps, to print out results and a listing of the program. Input and output of data to and from different devices need to be coordinated and errors in program execution must be detected and reported. These various tasks are directed by the *operating system* of the computer: a (frequently very large) set of programs controlling the use of the computer's resources.

By issuing commands, the programmer may communicate with the operating system. Thus, we can instruct the computer to run a program, for example, or to send the results to a particular output device. On the more primitive computers we may have to specify certain resource requirements for a program: its approximate storage requirements or the length of time needed to run it, for example. Unfortunately, although a Pascal program itself should run on any computer with a Pascal compiler, the dialogue between the user and the operating system varies substantially from computer to computer. As a result, the precise details of how to run a Pascal program on your specific computer will have to be determined from local documentation and we can refer in this book only in general terms to the interaction between Pascal and an operating system.

Exercises

4.1 Work through the 'black-box example' using the numbers 20, 30 and 40 presented to the input.

4.2 The following is a complete version of the Pascal program which was used to illustrate the action of the 'black-box' computer.

PROGRAM addthree(input,output);

VAR a, b, c, sum:integer;

```
BEGIN
    read(a);
    read(b);
    read(c);
    sum:=a+b+c;
    write(sum)
END.
```

Study the documentation on the computer system you will be using and carry out the following (you will need to become familiar with the commands to *input*, *edit*, *compile* and *run* the program):

(1) Input the program to a file on the computer.

(2) Compile the program.

(3) Run the program, entering the three numbers to be added together (separated by spaces and finishing with a newline), and observe the result.

(4) Alter the program (using the editor) so that the third number (c) is subtracted from the sum of the other two.

(5) Compile the new program and run it again.

Note: local variations may oblige certain rephrasing of the above steps.

First steps in Pascal programming

5.1 Pascal program construction

The overall shape of a Pascal program is illustrated in figure 5.1 in a form that will be used in later explanations to outline some of the Pascal constructions (the *syntax* of the language). This is a very simple notation which removes the risk of ambiguity that could tend to creep into a written description of the syntax and it has the added advantage of being concise. *Syntax diagrams*, as these are called, of the entire set of Pascal features occupy only a few pages in appendix 1. In the notation, the item being defined is on the left-hand side ('program' in figure 5.1), encircled symbols stand literally for the symbol enclosed and names in rectangular boxes represent items that are defined elsewhere, that is, in further syntax diagrams. Arrows between items imply a sequence and may be read as 'followed by'. Thus, it will be evident later that the example program in figure 5.2 conforms to the syntax of a 'program', since the first line is an example of a 'heading', everything between **begin** and **end** inclusive forms a 'block' and there is a full stop at the end.

A program heading is defined in figure 5.3. All programs start with the word 'program' followed by an identifier which is chosen by the programmer as a means of labelling a program for future reference (the exact form of an identifier is given in section 5.2). The items in brackets which follow this identifier specify the connection between the program and the world outside – the operating system of the computer. In the simple program of figure 5.2, for example, 'output' is written here to indicate that the program

Figure 5.1. Program syntax.

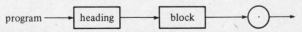

will send data out of the program. 'Input' will be included in later programs where data are also read into the program.

Figure 5.3 also introduces the idea of optional repetition into the notation. Inside the brackets we may select a single identifier by choosing the straight path, or an identifier followed by a comma followed by another identifier by looping back through the bottom branch. This looping may continue as many times as required, giving a syntax within the brackets which may be explained in words as 'a series of one or more identifiers separated by commas'. Similarly, the entire bracketed part of a program heading can be omitted in appropriate circumstances by following the 'bypass link' directly to the semicolon. It is most unusual, however, for a program heading not to contain at least 'output' unless the computer is controlling some equipment directly rather than displaying output to the user.

The word 'block' is a common one in programming and refers to a piece of program that is in some way complete. In figure 5.1, for example, the block referred to is indeed the entire program apart from the heading but, in general, we shall see that there may be other blocks within this 'outer' block, each complete in itself and each characterised by a surrounding **begin** and **end**.

Do not worry about the precise details in the syntax diagrams as they are introduced. Examples will always be given and the diagrams are mainly used as reference material when more experience has been gained in using the constructions. Note that some syntax diagrams in the text are simplified versions: the full ISO definition is given in appendix 1.

Figure 5.2. A simple program.

```
program sayhello(output);
begin
    write('hello')
end.
```

Figure 5.3. The program heading.

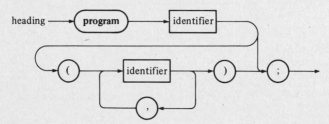

Some words in Pascal, such as **program**, **begin**, and **end** have special meaning to the compiler and are called *reserved words*. A programmer is free to choose names within a program to represent objects of data with the restriction that none of the reserved words of Pascal are used for this purpose. To avoid conflict, a list of these reserved words is given in appendix 2.

Throughout this book reserved words are printed in bold type to distinguish them from identifiers invented by the programmer and from standard identifiers of, for example, types such as 'integer' or 'real'. On most computer keyboards a convenient alternative is to use capital letters for the reserved words. This is not strictly necessary since the compiler recognises reserved words by context and not by typeface but the special significance of reserved words in the language deserves some recognition by the programmer and it is a good idea to distinguish them in program listings. Whether this is achieved by using capital letters or by some other means depends to a large extent on the character set of the input and output devices on the computer being used.

Program statements are written in free-format, meaning that in general, spaces and newlines are ignored by the compiler except within reserved words, identifiers and a few special compound symbols. Thus, we could write the heading of the program in figure 5.2 as

      program   sayhello (output);

or as

      program
              sayhello   (output);

or even as

      program
      sayhello
        (
            output
)
               ;

but not as

      pro
      gram say hello (output);

5.2   Identifiers and declarations

In chapter 2 we talked about data and the categorisation of data into data types. Within a Pascal program, all objects of data are associated with a specific data type by means of a *declaration*. An *identifier* is declared to represent the object and this must conform to the syntax in figure 5.4. Thus, an identifier is made up of a letter followed by zero or more letters and/or digits. Some legal identifiers are

        a
        k9
        r2d2
        size
        width

and some illegal ones:

1variable	– starts with a digit
step size	– 'space' not a letter/digit
lay-by	– neither is '-'

The intuitive meanings of 'letter' and 'digit' may be confirmed by reference to the syntax diagrams in appendix 1.

Note that the syntax of identifiers permits infinitely long identifiers since we can continue to go round the loop *ad infinitum*. In practice, very long identifiers will always be accepted by Pascal compilers but only a limited number of characters are usually considered as significant. If, for example, the first eight characters are significant then the identifiers

        plastic1
and
        plastic2

will be distinct, but not
        variable1
and
        variable2

Figure 5.4. Identifier.

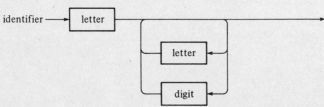

Choosing an identifier that fits the use to be made of it is very important, especially in a large program. Avoid the temptation to use large numbers of single letter identifiers such as a,b,c, etc. which do not reflect the meaning of the data item being represented. In a program to analyse a piece of text, for example, we should expect to find identifiers such as 'word', 'sentence', 'letter' or even 'punctuationmark' and such choices will assist considerably in 'self-documenting' your programs.

A *declaration* associates an identifier with a data type and this is always the first occurrence of that identifier in the program. Thus, the *variable declaration* whose syntax is given in figure 5.5 introduces identifiers of variables. For example, if we decide to use an integer variable called 'count' in a program it may be declared as

> **var** count:integer;

The reserved Pascal word **var** designates a variable declaration and the syntax demands a colon to separate the identifier from the data type.

Several identifiers of the same type may be introduced, separated by commas as in

> **var** count, index1, index2:integer;

As well as 'integer', the other three data types introduced in chapter 2 are available. They are called 'char', 'real' and 'Boolean', allowing declarations such as

> **var** count, index:integer;
> nextcharacter:char;
> endofword:Boolean;

Note that **var** is written just once and that the component declarations are separated by semicolons.

Referring back to the account of storage in the last chapter these variable declarations introduce the locations in the computer store (the 'pigeon-holes') into which we shall later place items of data of the type declared, with a unique identifier for each one.

Figure 5.5. Variable declaration.

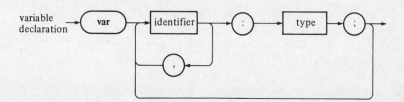

Not all data items used in a program are variable. Values known before the program is executed may be written as literal values, such as

2	– a literal integer
3.14159	– a literal real
'x'	– a literal char

The last of these, a literal char, is surrounded by primes to distinguish it from the identifier x.

In writing literals we are again constrained by a precise syntax. In the case of numbers, the syntax diagrams seem rather unwieldy (see appendix 1) but they confirm more or less what we would expect. A number may be a signed or unsigned series of decimal digits with or without a decimal point depending on the type. A few examples of signed literals are

$$\left.\begin{matrix} +65 \\ \\ -3999 \end{matrix}\right\} \text{integers} \qquad \left.\begin{matrix} +2.0 \\ \\ -5.66667 \end{matrix}\right\} \text{reals}$$

Note that the decimal point distinguishes, for example, the real number 2.0 from the integer 2 as discussed in chapter 2.

Each implementation of Pascal will impose a maximum size limit on integers and reals and also a precision for reals. This limit will vary depending on the particular computer used.

5.3   Statements

The steps in the program, that is, the instructions which actually express the algorithm, are written as *statements* in Pascal. Statements are executed by the computer in sequence, from the first onwards, except that some statements have the ability to modify this flow of control; to conditionally obey other statements or to repeat statements, for example. These 'control structures' are described in the next chapter.

The most common statement of all is the *assignment statement*. As its name suggests this is a way of assigning a value to a variable and its simple form is

variable: = expression

The ':=' is a compound symbol signifying assignment of the value on the right-hand side to the variable on the left-hand side. It is very important to distinguish this one way action from the notion of equality implied by the '=' operator. Pedantically, the action of assignment may be explained as

Evaluate the expression on the right-hand side and copy the resulting value into the location whose identifier is on the left-hand side.

Thus, there is no sense of testing for equality implied in assignment. Some examples are

    count:= 10
    nextcharacter:= poundsign
    index:= 2*count+1

It is helpful, perhaps, to read ':=' as 'becomes', as in 'count becomes 10' to emphasise the sense of assignment as a movement of the value 10 into the location identified by 'count'. Note that the left-hand side *must* be a single, suitable destination for the assignment, that is, an identifier. Thus, the following are meaningless:

    10:= count
    index+1:= count

It is quite common and perfectly sensible to write an assignment of the form

    count:= count+1

Here, as always, the action of the assignment is to evaluate the expression on the right-hand side (1 is added to the current value of 'count') and to place this value in the location identified by the left-hand side (which happens to be 'count' again). The effect is to increment the value of 'count' by 1.

5.4   Expressions

The expression on the right-hand side of an assignment statement may consist of a mixture of constants, identifiers and operators governed by the syntax of expressions, part of which is shown in figure 5.6.

Figure 5.6. Simple expression.

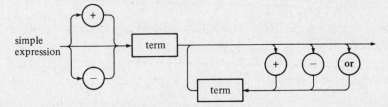

Briefly, a simple expression consists of one or more terms separated by the operators '+', '−' or '**or**'. A term is defined in figure 5.7 as a series of one or more factors separated by the operators shown and, finally, some of the possibilities for 'factor' are defined in figure 5.8.

The syntax appears rather complicated but in practice expressions look quite familiar as the examples below show.

        a+b
        −p*q
        x*y+3
        length*width
        (b*b−4*a*c)/(2*a)

The important characteristics of expression syntax compared to more usual algebraic notation may be summed up as follows:

Figure 5.7. Term.

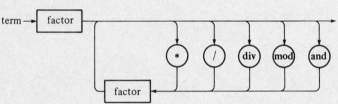

Figure 5.8. Factor.

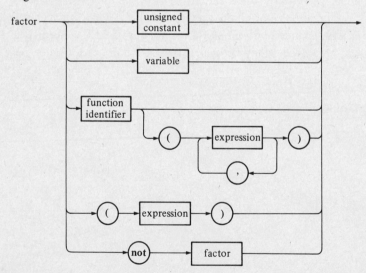

1. The multiplication symbol, '*', conventionally omitted in algebra (for example, ab+c), must always be inserted in an expression (thus, a*b+c).

2. The expression must be written one character after another along the line. Division is expressed by the symbol '/'; for example,

   p/q

   as opposed to

   $$\frac{p}{q}$$

3. An order of precedence is implied in evaluating an expression. This usually matches the intuitive algebraic scheme such that in an expression like a+b*c the multiplication is performed first giving an elaboration equivalent to a+(b*c) rather than to (a+b)*c. Similarly, it must be remembered that

   x+y/2

   is equivalent to

   $$x+\frac{y}{2}$$

   and not to

   $$\frac{x+y}{2}$$

   since division takes precedence over addition.

The precedence of all the operators is inherent in the syntax diagrams but it is expanded into tabular form in figure 5.9 for convenience. Any of these precedences may be overridden by the use of brackets; hence,

   (x+y)/2

is equivalent to

$$\frac{x+y}{2}$$

Figure 5.9. Precedence of operators.

operator	precedence
not	first
* / **div mod and**	second
+ − **or**	third
<= < = <> > >=	fourth

and brackets may be nested to any depth; for example,

$$(a-(b+c))*d$$

Note that operators of the same precedence are evaluated from left to right, thus

$$a/b*2$$

is equivalent to

$$\frac{2a}{b}$$

and not

$$\frac{a}{2b}$$

Two operators, **div** and **mod** are designed specifically to operate on integers:

i **div** j means divide i by j and truncate (lose remainder)

For example, 11 **div** 3 is equal to 3 (remainder 2 lost).

a **mod** b means a modulo b (the remainder after **div**)
= a−a **div** b*b (b must be positive).

Every expression delivers a result of a particular data type which is determined by the operators used and, perhaps, by the types of the operands (the values operated on). In arithmetic expressions it is acceptable in some circumstances to mix integers and real values and there are three simple rules to determine the data type of the result:

1. With the operators '+', '−' and '*', the result will be *real* unless all operands are integer in which case the result is *integer*.

2. With '/' the result will always be *real*.

3. With **div** and **mod** the operands and result are always *integer*.

In practice, in an expression such as

$$10*3.3$$

where one operand is integer and the other real, then the integer operand will be converted to real before the multiplication is performed. Thus, we may consider the above as a reasonable abbreviation of

$$10.0*3.3$$

Note that despite the fact that the result of this expression is 33.0, a whole number, the result is still a real number.

Division is rather different in that two integer operands produce a real result if the operator '/' is used. Thus, 10/4 gives 2.5 and 10/5 gives 2.0, a real number. The integer operator **div** is used if the integer result of division is required.

Whereas conversion of an integer to a real value is automatic within expressions, conversion the other way round, that is, real to integer, is never performed automatically. For example, in an assignment to determine the approximate equivalent value in degrees centigrade of a temperature in degrees fahrenheit we may *not* use

$$degreec := (degreef - 32)*5/9$$

('degreec' and 'degreef' of type integer). The division operator used in this expression implies that a real result will be delivered and this may not be assigned to an integer variable ('degreec'). The reason for this is that the effect would be ambiguous – do we wish the answer to be the *nearest* integer value or, perhaps, the largest integer value *not greater than* the real result? Here, we may well decide that the conversion required is to 'round' the real result to the nearest integer degree and we must force this by using a special 'standard function' as described in the next section.

5.5 Standard functions

A branch of the syntax chart in figure 5.8 allows the use of standard functions in expressions. These may be used to perform some of the more commonly required tasks such as finding square roots and trigonometrical functions (sin, cos etc.) as in

$$e := m*sqr(c)$$
$$root := sqrt(num)$$

The standard functions require an argument – the value upon which the function will operate – and this is written in brackets following the name of the function. The result delivered by the function may be used in the same way as any other value in an expression. A list of standard functions and the types of their argument and results is given in appendix 3.

In general, the argument to a function may be any expression delivering a result of the correct type. Hence, we could write

$$y := sqrt(2*x + 5)$$

and we may 'nest' calls on standard functions as in

$$c := sqrt(sqr(a) + sqr(b))$$

In all cases the expression making up the argument to the function is worked out to give a single value to which the function is applied.

Two of the standard functions in appendix 3, 'trunc' and 'round', are called transfer functions since a real argument is converted to an integer result in each case. Thus, in the temperature conversion example earlier, if we decide that it is most sensible to 'round' the real result to the nearest integer value we can use

degreec: = round((degreef − 32)∗5/9)

Alternatively, if we insist on a value in degrees centigrade that is on no account greater than the real result then the result is given by

degreec: = trunc((degreef − 32)∗5/9)

The functions 'ord' and 'chr' may be unfamiliar. With a variable 'x' of type char, 'ord(x)' returns the integer corresponding to the position of that character in the character set (its *ord*inal position); 'chr' works the other way round, returning the character whose ordinal position is supplied as the (integer) argument. As mentioned before, the actual ordering of the character set may vary from implementation to implementation, but since the digits are guaranteed to be in order and consecutive we can use 'ord' to give us the integer corresponding to a digit that has been read in as a character, for example:

x: = ord(dig) − ord('0')

where 'x' is an integer and 'dig' is of type char, and vice versa:

dig: = chr(x + ord('0'))

Note finally on this issue that the word 'parameter' is often used in computing circles instead of 'argument' and we shall prefer this alternative in some later discussions.

5.6   Boolean expressions

The inclusion of the three logical operators **and**, **or** and **not** in the syntax of expressions is perhaps less familiar to readers than the numerical operators. We are used to expressions that deliver an integer or real result but there is no reason why expressions may not be written that deliver a Boolean result of 'true' or 'false'. Thus, given a declaration of Boolean variables

var sunny, cloudy, rain, snow, ice: Boolean;

and assuming they are given suitable values (two special identifiers 'true' and 'false' are available to do this; for example, sunny:= true) then we may write expressions using the logical operators to make assignments to other Boolean variables (whose declarations are assumed here) such as

wetday:= rain
baddrivingconditions:= snow **or** ice
funnyweather:= sunny **and** rain
clearsky:= **not** cloudy

The precise meanings of the operators **and**, **or** and **not** are best explained using a truth table (figure 5.10) to show all possible combinations of values for two Boolean operands 'p' and 'q' with these operators. Briefly, 'p **and** q' is true if and only if *both* 'p' and 'q' are true whereas 'p **or** q' is true if *either* 'p' or 'q' or both are true; '**not** p' gives the complement of 'p' (false if 'p' is true and vice versa).

In accordance with the rules of precedence for operators we may combine logical operators as in

oddconditions:= **not** cloud **and** rain
dryday:= **not**(rain **or** snow)

A series of *relational operators* (figure 5.11) to compare non-Boolean operands and deliver a Boolean result, is provided.

Figure 5.10. Truth table.

possible combinations of values
and their results

p	true	true	false	false
q	true	false	true	false
p **and** q	true	false	false	false
p **or** q	true	true	true	false
not p	false	false	true	true

Figure 5.11. Relational operators.

=	equal
< >	not equal
<	less than
>	greater than
< =	less than or equal
> =	greater than or equal

Given an integer variable 'temperature' we may write an expression such as

temperature < 0

which will be 'true' or 'false' according to the value of 'temperature'. By combining these relational operators with the logical operators we may develop quite complex Boolean expressions:

ice: = (rain **or** snow) **and** (temperature < 32)
niceday: = sunny **and not** rain **and** (temperature $> = 70$)

being careful to watch the precedence of each of these operators and to include brackets to override undesirable ones.

Relational operators may also be used between character values, as in

ch = 'A'   {where 'ch' is of type char}
ch $< >$ '.'
(ch $> =$ 'a') **and** (ch $< =$ 'z')

'Less than' and 'greater than' operators should be interpreted as meaning 'earlier in the character set' or 'later in the character set' respectively, in the context of character comparison. Hence, the last of the above expressions will be 'true' if 'ch' is a lower-case alphabetic character, subject to possible variations in character set ordering mentioned later.

It may not be immediately clear why we should wish to write Boolean expressions at all. However, we shall see in the next chapter that they play a particularly important role in making up control statements.

5.7   Reading and writing

Every sensible program needs to communicate in some way with the world outside the computer; to read in data, perhaps, and certainly to write out at least one result. This is achieved most simply in Pascal by means of a pair of statements called 'read' and 'write'. At 'run-time', that is, when the computer is actually obeying the program, values may be given to variables in the program by the read statement. For example,

read(length)

(where 'length' is assumed here to be a 'real' variable) requires that an actual value for 'length' be provided when this statement is obeyed. In the case of a user running the Pascal program from a terminal connected directly to the computer, for example, this datum value could be provided by typing in a number for 'length' at the keyboard.

Several values may be read in the same read statement, as in

read(length, width)

and, in the case of numerical data, the values must be separated from each other by at least one space or begin on a 'newline' (additional spaces and new lines will be ignored).

When reading a character value, however, the very next character is retrieved from the input by a statement such as

read(nextchar)   {where 'nextchar' is a char variable}

remembering that a space will be treated in the same way as any other character.

Values are output from a Pascal program by the write statement as in

write(area)   {a real variable, say}

As in the case of the read statement, several items can be output in a single 'write' and, in general, an item may be any expression; for example,

write(length, width, length*width)

Output may be annotated by including a piece of text (a 'string of characters' in computing terms) in the statement enclosed in single quotes, as in

write('Area = ', area)

Data output using 'write' will all appear on the same line. A similar statement called 'writeln' is provided which behaves in exactly the same way as 'write' except that a new line is taken after the data have been output.

Finally, if a program uses 'read', the word 'input' should appear in the program heading as mentioned earlier. Similarly, the word 'output' should appear if data are to be output using 'write' or 'writeln'.

This brief introduction to input and output provides a sufficient base for writing the simple examples in the next couple of chapters. We shall return to take a more detailed look at Pascal input and output facilities later.

5.8   Semicolons and compound statements

As mentioned earlier, Pascal programs are written in free-format. Statements may stretch over several lines and they may contain spaces as desired, except within identifiers, reserved words and compound symbols such as ':='. In the light of this, in order to distinguish one statement from the following one a *semicolon* is used as a statement separator. A simple program will illustrate this:

```
program areaofrectangle (input,output);
var length, width, area:real;
begin
   read(length,width);
   area: = length*width;
   write('Area = ', area)
end.
```

The three statements of this program, between **begin** and **end**, are separated by two semicolons. Notice that neither the **begin** nor the statement immediately before **end** are followed by semicolons since **begin** and **end** are *not* statements (they are reserved words) and the semicolon is only used in *separating* statements.

One of the most powerful features of Pascal is the ability to write *compound statements*. A compound statement has the syntax shown in figure 5.12: basically, one or more statements separated by semicolons and enclosed by **begin** and **end**. We shall see shortly that there are statements that perform certain actions on other statements: conditionally obeying or repeating a statement, for example. Add to this the general rule that permits us to use a compound statement wherever a single statement is allowed, and the range of possible constructions is considerably enhanced.

Figure 5.12. Compound statement.

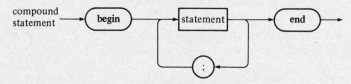

5.9   A short program

Using the statements introduced in this chapter it is now possible to write simple but complete programs. As an example, the program below performs the simple task of reading a value and the current VAT rate and of printing the VAT and total price.

```
program vatcalc (input, output);
var vat, vatrate, basic:real;
```

begin
    write('Enter basic value and VAT rate:');
    read(basic, vatrate);
    vat: = basic * vatrate / 100;
    writeln('Basic = ', basic, ' VAT rate = ', vatrate);
    writeln('VAT = ', vat, ' total = ', basic + vat)
end.

If you try this program, do not be put off by the awkward way in which the numbers are printed out. We shall see how to make the output look much neater in chapter 8. In common with most programs in this book this one is written with the *interactive* user in mind. By 'interactive' here we imply that the user is seated at a terminal that is connected directly ('online') to the computer so that when a program is running, data are typed in from the terminal and results are sent directly to the terminal. Thus, in this and many later programs we output a 'prompt' message to the terminal to request data to be entered. Prompts of this kind would be omitted in a non-interactive environment.

Exercises

5.1 Which of the following are not legal Pascal declarations and why?

    (*a*) **var**   a, b1, c-2:real;
    (*b*) **var**   myid1:integer, myid2:char;
    (*c*) **var**   count, sum, number:integer;
                    ch, nextch:char; flag:boolean;

5.2 Explain in words the definition of 'oddherd' in the syntax diagram below.

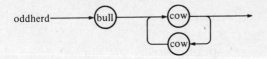

5.3 Draw a syntax diagram to define the following:
A library number consists of the letter 'A', 'B' or 'C' followed by one or more digits separated from each other by hyphens. An optional letter 'L' may be placed after the last digit.
(Examples of library numbers are A2L, A1-3-2, C2-6-3-5.)

5.4 Write expressions for the following (assume suitable declarations):

(a) $\dfrac{2x+y}{3}$ (b) $\sqrt{(\frac{1}{2}p-q)}$ (c) $(a+2)(b-3)$

5.5 Write Boolean expressions which are true when the value of:

(*a*) the integer 'double' is twice as big as the integer 'single';

(*b*) the integer 'watertemp' is between 0 and 100 inclusive;

(*c*) the char variable 'ch' is not a vowel;

(*d*) the integer 'm' is exactly divisible by 3 (hint: use **mod**).

5.6 In a program to process sales accounts a programmer identifies a set of variables which includes the following:

(*a*) 'intotal' – an invoice total in pounds and pence;

(*b*) 'innumber' – the invoice number;

(*c*) 'vatrate' – the current VAT rate;

(*d*) 'goodsent' – to mark that the associated goods have been dispatched;

(*e*) 'factory' – a single letter code identifying the product source.

Write down suitable Pascal declarations for the above variables.

Control structures

A program consisting entirely of statements that are obeyed sequentially as in the example at the end of the last chapter is rarely of any practical use. Since each statement is obeyed once only it is invariably faster to perform the calculation on a calculator rather than go to the trouble of writing a program. The real benefit of a computer is only apparent when we introduce statements that can modify this sequential obeying of statements: the *control structures* of Pascal.

In terms of the order in which statements are obeyed in a program we may identify three categories:

> Sequence
> Condition
> Repetition

The assignment statement, and read and write statements previously introduced are examples of sequential programming steps.

6.1   Conditional statements

Sometimes we only want to execute a statement, or a set of statements, if a given condition prevails and, perhaps, to execute a different statement if that condition does not arise. A conditional statement enabling us to do this is outlined in figure 6.1.

The statement following the reserved word **then** will be obeyed if, and only if, the Boolean expression following the **if** is 'true' and similarly, the statement following **else** is only obeyed if the expression yields 'false'.

For example, if the three variables 'large', 'first' and 'second' are all integer, then to assign to 'large' the larger of the two integers 'first' and 'second' we may write

> **if** first > second
> **then** large:= first
> **else** large:= second

There is an absence of semicolons within this statement. The terms **then** and **else** are reserved words, not statements, and thus they do not (must not) involve the use of the statement separator ';'.

The Boolean expression itself may be as complicated as desired, using the logical operators **and, or** and **not** where necessary to combine elements, as in

> **if** (colour = red) **or** (colour = yellow) **or** (colour = blue)
> **then** write('Primary')
> **else** write('Not primary')

(We shall assume relevant declarations and previous assignments to variables in this and the next few examples.)

Note the use of brackets here to override the precedence of the **or** operator which is greater than that of the '=' operator.

From the syntax diagram it can be seen that the **else** part of the statement is optional. If there is no sensible alternative action to the **then** proposed we omit the **else** altogether. For example,

> **if** (fish = trout) **and** (fishlength > sizelimit)
> **then** write('Trout for dinner')

Here, if the Boolean expression yields 'false', the statement following **then** is not obeyed and control passes immediately to the next statement in the program.

The apparent restriction in the syntax of only a single statement following a **then** or an **else** is not serious. One example of a 'statement' is the compound statement introduced earlier. Thus, we may group together many statements into a single compound statement as shown in the following example:

Figure 6.1. Conditional statement.

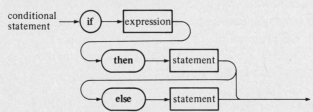

```
if fish = salmon
  then begin
         tackle:= heavy;
         write('No work today')
       end
```

In addition, a statement within the **if** may itself be another conditional statement, as in

```
if ship = sloop
  then masts:= 1
  else if ship = ketch
         then masts:= 2
         else if ship = schooner
                then masts:= 3
```

Including further control structures within others in this manner is called *nesting* and may be continued to any depth.

The indented layout of the above conditional statements is not mandatory in the sense that the compiler ignores spacing and newline information in performing its translation process. Thus, as far as the compiler is concerned, we could have written the last example as

```
if ship = sloop then masts:= 1 else if
ship = ketch then masts:= 2 else if
ship = schooner then masts:= 3
```

Layout is extremely important, however, from the viewpoint of program readability. It is vital to adopt a consistent convention for all statements that shows clearly the structure of those statements. In the second format above, the structure (which **then**s and **else**s belong to which **if**s, for example) is obscured by bad layout. Precise conventions for layout tend to vary quite substantially according to individual preferences but two general rules are recommended:

1. *Indentation*
   Each new compound statement, block or component of a control statement should be drawn to the reader's attention by indentation in the program listing. Thus, in the first nested example above, each **then** and associated **else** is indented to the right of the corresponding **if**.

2. *Matching pairs*
   Every **end** should be placed vertically below its matching **begin**.

Since any further **begins** and **ends** in between the two will be indented to the right it is then an easy matter to match up corresponding **begins** and **ends** – most helpful in understanding the action of a section of program. The same principle can be extended to pairs of **thens** and **elses** so that, again, a **then** and its corresponding **else** will be found in the same vertical line for ease of visual matching.

Example
A program to determine if a given year is a leap year.

Since the Gregorian calendar was introduced in 1752 a leap year occurs once every 4 years, except that the century year is only leap once every 400 years (in fact, a further correction is applied every 4000th year, but we shall ignore that here!).

To turn this description into an algorithm it is actually rather simpler to turn the argument round and test initially for the 400 year case before the more frequently occurring 4 year case (try the other way to convince yourself).

The algorithm is:

> If the year is divisible by 400
>   then it is leap
>   else if the year is divisible by 4 and not by 100
>   then it is leap
>   else it is not leap.

If we choose an identifier 'year' to represent the year in question then its data type is clearly integer. We can determine whether an integer is divisible by another by using **mod**, the integer operator that gives the remainder after dividing by another integer. If a year *is* divisible by 4, for example, then the remainder must be zero and hence the following Boolean expression will be true:

> year **mod** 4 = 0

Introducing a Boolean variable 'leap' to hold the result we may construct a complete conditional statement from the above algorithm:

> **if** year **mod** 400 = 0
> **then** leap: = true
> **else if** (year **mod** 4 = 0) **and not** (year **mod** 100 = 0)
>   **then** leap: = true
>   **else** leap: = false

Note that the indentation of this statement conforms to the general rule mentioned above in placing **else**s directly beneath the corresponding **then**s. Also, the brackets used in the Boolean expression of the nested **if** are necessary because of the precedences of the component operators. A complete program to read in a year and print out whether it is leap is given below.

```
program leapyear (input, output);
var  year:integer;
     leap:Boolean;
begin
  write('Enter year');
  read(year);
  if year mod 400 = 0
    then leap:= true
    else if (year mod 4 = 0) and not (year mod 100 = 0)
            then leap:= true
            else leap:= false;
  if leap
    then write('This is a leap year')
    else write('This is not a leap year')
end.
```

The use of a Boolean variable, 'leap' in this example, to mark that an event has, or has not occurred (here, that a year is leap or not leap) is common in programming. This use is rather like that of a flag which may be raised to signify an event. Although a good example to illustrate the use of conditional statements, it is left to the reader to verify that in this particular case the main **if** statement may be replaced by a single assignment statement:

$$\text{leap}:= (\text{year } \mathbf{mod}\ 400 = 0)\ \mathbf{or}\ (\text{year } \mathbf{mod}\ 4 = 0)$$
$$\mathbf{and\ not}\ (\text{year } \mathbf{mod}\ 100 = 0)$$

Note finally that this program would need revision before it could be released for general use. There are at present no checks placed on the input data, allowing, for instance, a date previous to the introduction of the present calendar to be analysed. Rigorous checking of data is most important in any program that is to be used seriously. It is most unfortunate that the lack of space and desire to concentrate on particular constructions in this and other programming texts oblige the authors to omit so much of this extra coding.

6.2   Repetition

Much of the power of a computer is derived from its ability to repeat statements many times and very rapidly. The conditions under which statements may be repeated fall into several general categories, with Pascal providing three separate mechanisms for constructing *loops*, the name given to this repetitive process.

Figure 6.2 gives the syntax of the first loop construction, the **while** statement.

The term **while** should be interpreted as 'as long as', in this usage, since the statement following the word **do** is repeated for as long as the expression following **while** evaluates to 'true' (clearly it must be a Boolean expression). The action of the **while** statement is as follows. On first entry to the loop the expression is evaluated and if true, the statement following the **do** is obeyed. Following this, the expression is evaluated again and if it still yields true the statement is obeyed a second time and so on. When the expression is checked and yields false, control passes to the next statement below the **while**.

As before, the statement in the loop may be a compound statement enclosing a section of program to be repeated.

For example, to read characters one by one and count the number of letter 'z's until a full stop is encountered, we may use the following:

```
read(nextchar);
while nextchar < > '.' do
   begin
     if nextchar = 'z'
        then zcount: = zcount + 1;
     read(nextchar)
   end
```

assuming that 'nextchar' and 'zcount' have been declared previously as char and integer variables, respectively and that 'zcount' is set to zero before the loop is entered. Adding one to its value within the loop, whenever a letter 'z' is encountered steadily accumulates the correct count in 'zcount'.

It is particularly useful to employ **while** loops to read in values up to a predetermined terminator (a full stop above). Often, a suitable terminator

Figure 6.2. **while** statement.

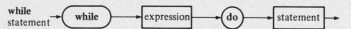

for input is the end of a line and Pascal provides a special identifier 'eoln', of type Boolean, which is set to 'true' whenever the end of a line is encountered in reading; 'eoln' is automatically accessible in all programs without need for declaration. Here is the outline of a loop that reads characters up to the end of the current line:

```
while not eoln do
  begin
    read(nextchar);
    .
    .            {process nextchar}
    .
  end
```

As a more complete example, the following program reads characters up to the end of a line and prints out the number of spaces encountered:

```
program countspaces (input, output);

var  spaces:integer;
     nextchar:char;
begin
  spaces:= 0;
  while not eoln do
    begin
      read(nextchar);
      if nextchar = '   '
        then spaces:= spaces+1
    end;
  write(spaces,'spaces encountered')
end.
```

The syntax of a second loop construction is shown in figure 6.3.

The **repeat** statement is similar in action to **while**. The statement or statements following the reserved word **repeat** are repeated until the Boolean expression after **until** becomes 'true'. The main difference is that

Figure 6.3. **repeat** statement.

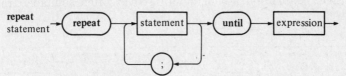

in the **repeat** statement the test is carried out at the end of the loop as opposed to at the beginning in the case of **while**. Because of this the loop will always be obeyed at least once, whereas with **while**, if the expression is 'false' on first entry the loop is not obeyed at all and control passes immediately to the next statement.

Using **repeat** we could write a similar sequence to the first 'eoln' example above:

> **repeat**
>   read(nextchar);
>
>   .
>   .   {process nextchar}
>   .
>
> **until** eoln

But note that this will not have the same effect as a **while** version if 'eoln' is true on first entry since it will cause the statements in the loop to be obeyed once even in this case. We must take this characteristic into account when selecting a loop construction.

The third looping device is the **for** statement, whose syntax is defined in figure 6.4 and this is rather different to the other two.

The **for** statement uses a *control variable* which takes on successive values each time through the loop. For example, on entry to the **for** statement

> **for** number: = 1 **to** 10 **do**
>   write(number)

where the control variable 'number' is of type integer, 'number' is set to the first value '1'. This value is then checked against the final value after **to** and since it is less than or equal to this value (10) the statement following **do** is executed. Following this, 'number' is incremented by 1 and compared to the final value again and the loop repeated a second time. This continues

Figure 6.4. **for** statement.

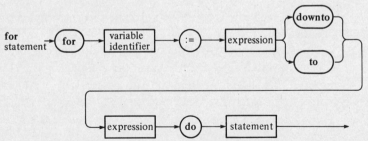

until 'number' is found to exceed 10 in the test. In other words, the loop will be obeyed 10 times with 'number' taking on successive values from 1 to 10.

The control variable is available for use within the loop. The next example uses this facility to print the squares of numbers from 1 to 10:

> **for** value: = 1 **to** 10 **do**
>   writeln(value,sqr(value))

In general, the starting and finishing values for the loop control variable may be any expression. Modifying the above loop to

> **for** value: = first **to** last **do**
>   writeln(value,sqr(value))

enables printing of any series of values and their squares by arranging for 'first' and 'last' to take values read in as data, for example.

In place of **to** we may substitute **downto**, in which case 1 is subtracted from the control variable each time round. Also, the control variable may be of a type other than integer (though not real). In particular, we may step a control variable through successive values in the character set using a **for** statement in the style of

> **for** nextchar: = 'a' **to** 'z' **do** ...

Though the ordering of a character set is the prerogative of the computer manufacturer it is a safe bet to assume that the alphabetic characters are consecutive in the character set and that this **for** statement will cause the loop to be obeyed 26 times.

Finally, a few observations concerning the use of the control variable:

1. The value of the control variable should never be changed within the loop.
2. The loop will not be obeyed at all if the initial value exceeds the final value on first entry (if the initial value is less than the final value in the case of **downto**).
3. On exit from the loop the value of the control variable becomes undefined.
4. ISO-Pascal imposes restrictions on the declaration and use of control variables in order to assist the compiler in detecting and preventing illegal modifications to this variable within a loop. Thus, it is safer, and usually clearer when writing a **for** loop to declare a variable and reserve it for use as the control variable in this loop and for no other purpose.

6.3   Choosing loop structures

Choosing the correct loop structure to use in any application depends largely on the conditions under which that loop is to be repeated. The initial choice is between a **for** statement and the **while/repeat–until** pair, since these are used in very different circumstances:

> A **for** statement is used when the number of times the loop is to be repeated is known *before entry* to the loop.

> A **while** or **repeat–until** statement is chosen when the number of times the loop is to be repeated is determined *within the loop* and is not known on entry.

Example

To illustrate this difference consider the problem of reading a series of numbers and calculating their average.

If we have a known number of numbers, say 20, then the most suitable loop is a **for** loop as shown in the program below.

```
program findaverage (input, output);

var  average, nextnum, sum:real;
     count:integer;
begin
   sum:= 0;
   for count:= 1 to 20 do
     begin
        read(nextnum);
        sum:= sum+nextnum
     end;
   average:= sum/20;
   write(average)
end.
```

Here, although the control variable 'count' is not used in the loop, a **for** statement is clearly demanded since it is known that precisely 20 iterations (repetitions) of the loop are required. In fact, the program could be made more generally useful by preceding the data by the number of numbers and then reading in this value. At the point in the program where the loop is entered, however, the number of iterations would by then be known (by reading in the value) and a **for** statement would still be the most suitable choice.

On the other hand, suppose the data were organised such that the number of numbers was not readily available at the time of input. This could occur, for example, if there were too many numbers to count easily. An alternative approach to the averaging problem is to use a special terminator at the end of the data and to continue reading and summing numbers until this terminator is found.

In the following program it is assumed that the last number in the data is followed by a negative number. This implies that negative numbers may not form part of the data themselves and that we may interpret this negative value as the terminator. In practice, we may need to seek a less restrictive value for this purpose.

```
program anotheraverage (input, output);
var  average, nextnum, sum:real;
     count:integer;
begin
  sum:= 0;
  count:= 0;
  read(nextnum);
  while nextnum > = 0 do
    begin
      sum:= sum + nextnum;
      count:= count + 1;
      read(nextnum)
    end;
  average:= sum/count;
  write(average)
end.
```

This time the loop must be a **while** or **repeat–until** because the number of times it is to be obeyed is not known at the outset. A **while** statement is preferred on the grounds that the terminator may possibly occur as the first number and this contingency cannot be catered for naturally using a **repeat–until** construction with the conditional test at the end of the loop. Note, however, that as it stands this program will still fail if there are no numbers since the expression

sum/count

should produce an error message at run-time if count is zero. Dividing a number by zero causes *arithmetic overflow*, a condition that can be detected by the computer. A more rigorous program must check for this eventuality and a suitable modification is left as an exercise for the reader.

6.4   **The case statement**

Statements of the general form

if i = value1
    then statement1
    else if i = value2
         then statement2
         else if i = value3 etc.

where 'i' is an integer variable and 'value1', 'value2', etc. are constants, occur quite frequently. The **case** statement generalises the notion of conditional selection of statements to enable the above relationship to be expressed more neatly as

    case i **of**
      value1: statement1;
      value2: statement2;
      value3: statement3;

         .

         .

         .

      valueN: statementN
    end

The value of the *case selector* ('i') must always match just one of the constants within the **case** and this determines uniquely which statement is obeyed. The syntax of **case** is given in figure 6.5.

The syntax permits more than one constant to be associated with a statement. Items in such lists are separated by commas. As before, any of the statements in the **case** may be compound statements.

Figure 6.5. **case** statement.

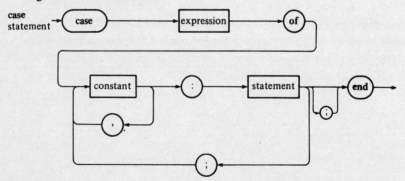

As an example, consider a program to calculate the number of days in a given month. We shall assume that the year is not a leap year!

Having read in the month as an integer between 1 and 12 we could employ a conditional statement to test this month number against all possibilities, as in

> **if** (month = 9) **or** (month = 4) **or** (month = 6) **or** (month = 11)
>   **then** days: = 30
>   **else if** month = 2
>   **then** days: = 28
>   **else** days: = 31

which is a formal representation of the well-known rule 'Thirty days have September etc.'. Noting the similarity between the expressions in the above **if**s (they all involve the same identifier on the left-hand side and a constant on the right-hand side), we may replace this conditional statement by a **case** statement:

> **case** month **of**
>   9,4,6,11: days: = 30;
>   2: days: = 28;
>   1,3,5,7,8,10,12: days: = 31
> **end**

Although every value for 'month' must be entered explicitly in this construction, the relationship between a value for 'month' and the number of days in that month is shown much more clearly in the **case** statement. Just one of the statements will be obeyed, depending on the value of 'month'. Note that all possible values *are* catered for since an error will result from entering a **case** statement with a value that is not found as one of the constants.

The convention of indenting has been continued with all conditional and looping constructions as a distinct aid to program readability. Thus, the statements in each new loop, either **for, while** or **repeat–until** are indented, as are those in a **case**, with matching pairs (for example, **case–end**) always written in the same vertical line.

Exercises

6.1 Modify program 'leapyear' to print out a warning message for dates earlier than 1752.

6.2 Write Pascal statements to exchange the values in two integer variables ('a' and 'b') unless they are equal.

6.3 Write an **if** or a **case** statement, whichever is more appropriate, to perform the following tasks:

(*a*) Write out the number (between 0 and 9) in the integer variable 'dig' as a word (for example, 'three');
(*b*) Given three integer variables, 'a', 'b', and 'c', each of which contains a different positive value, write out the name of the variable which contains the smallest value;
(*c*) Write out a message to say if the 'char' variable 'symbol' contains a consonant, a vowel, or a non-alphabetic character.

6.4 Write a program that will find and print the largest of 20 numbers typed in. (Hint: use program 'findaverage' as an outline.)

6.5 Write a program to read in an integer between 1 and 4 inclusive and print out the name of a vehicle with that many wheels.

6.6 Write sequences of statements to set the integer variable 'sum' equal to

(*a*) the sum of the first n natural numbers (that is, $1+2+3+ \ldots +n$)
(*b*) the sum of the first n even numbers (that is, $2+4+6+ \ldots +2n$)

6.7 Write a 'one-arm bandit' program that will read in three characters representing the three reel positions across the 'win' line and pay out (as a printed IOU!) 10p if the first two symbols are the same and 20p if all three are the same. For example,

AAA   payout 20p
PPL   payout 10p
APA   no payout

6.8 Modify the 'bandit' program in exercise 6.7 so that the game repeats until a line of asterisks ('***') is entered. Keep a running total of the sum of money won or lost so far, printing this out after each 'spin'.

Procedures and functions

'Procedure' is the name given in many programming languages to a self-contained section of a program which can be included in a complete program. Two examples of procedures in Pascal are 'read' and 'write' which were introduced earlier to perform input and output of values. With these two, the 'self-contained' sequences of instructions which perform the input and output have been written by the Pascal system implementers and are completely hidden from the user. They are called 'standard' procedures since they are available in all Pascal programs without the need for introduction.

However, we are not limited to using only standard procedures in programs since the facility exists in Pascal to define new procedures at the head of a program and to refer to them (technically, to 'call' them) later in the program. This is a powerful and useful concept.

7.1   Declaring and calling procedures

Making up and using a procedure in Pascal takes place in two parts, which are (1) a *procedure declaration*, in which a new procedure is defined and (2) one or more *procedure calls* that cause the procedure to be obeyed. In this way, a clear distinction is drawn between defining the action of a procedure and actually executing the statements in the definition. A simple example will help to make this distinction clear.

Suppose, for egotistical or other reasons, we would like to place a distinctive personal logo at the head of output from our programs using a sequence of write statements containing character strings to print, say, an initial enclosed in a diamond:

Rather than place the write statements directly into the program after the first **begin**, we may declare a **procedure** at the top of the program as follows:

```
program egotrip(output);

< any var declarations for the main program >

procedure logoprint;
begin
  writeln('           ^           ');
  writeln('          / \          ');
  writeln('         / c c c \         ');
  writeln('        / c \        ');
  writeln('        \ c /        ');
  writeln('         \ c c c /         ');
  writeln('          \ /          ');
  writeln('           v           ')
end;
```

Note that so far we are still in the declaration part of the program. A procedure *declaration* always starts with the word **procedure** followed by an identifier chosen by the programmer according to the usual rules. The actual statements to be obeyed when the procedure is called are enclosed by **begin** and **end**. The main part of the program is as follows:

```
begin
  logoprint;
  (other program statements if any)
end.
```

Thus, the action of printing the logo is initiated by simply writing the name of the procedure as a statement in the program itself. This procedure *call* has exactly the same effect as if the write statements were written in place of 'logoprint' at this point. However, since the above use of a procedure has brought about a lengthening of the program we ought really to stop for a moment and think what, if anything, has been achieved:

1. At any later stage in the program we can print a further copy of the logo by a single short statement.
2. The declaration of 'logoprint' is clearly distinct from the main program statements and can be taken out and used in other programs very easily.
3. By removing the detailed part of printing a logo to a procedure declaration the main program is rendered less cluttered and hence more readable.

In many applications of procedures it is this third point that is the most important of all. Procedures can be used to separate single, easily identifiable tasks from the body of a program and in this way enhance the ease with which that program can be written and understood. It is also much easier to test and remove errors from a large program if it is made up of logically distinct units in this way. We shall return to this important aspect of program design later.

Procedure declarations are written before the **begin** of the main program but after any **var** declarations. A program may contain any number of procedure declarations and the formal syntax is shown in figure 7.1.

In the simple example of 'logoprint', the 'parameter list' is empty and the 'block' consists of statements separated by semicolons and surrounded by **begin** and **end**. A glance at the syntax diagrams confirms, however, that a 'block' is in fact the syntax of an entire program after the heading, which makes the range of constructions available within a procedure very wide. It means, for example, that a procedure declaration may contain the declarations of other procedures which are called from within that procedure.

7.2 Local variables

Procedure 'logoprint' is unusual in that it does not involve the use of any variables. In fact, text output procedures are among the few sensible ones in which this is true. When a variable is required *that is only ever used*

Figure 7.1. Procedure declaration.

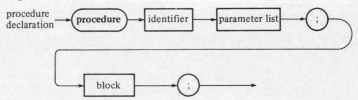

within that procedure, it can be declared at the top of that procedure in exactly the same way as in a **var** declaration in a program.

We can illustrate this with the following procedure which skips over characters at the input until a full stop is found:

```
procedure skiptonextsentence;
var ch:char;
begin
  repeat
    read(ch)
  until ch = '.'
end;
```

The object of this procedure is to 'throw away' all remaining characters in the current sentence, so that the next character read after calling the procedure will be the first after a full stop. Thus, the char variable 'ch' is used exclusively inside the procedure to test a character read from the input. Any value given to 'ch' is never used elsewhere in the program.

By declaring 'ch' at the top of the procedure declaration we have made 'ch' *local* to procedure 'skiptonextsentence'. It means that the existence of the char variable 'ch' is limited strictly to within this procedure and, hence, that 'ch' will 'disappear' when a procedure call is completed. Since 'ch' is only ever used within the procedure shown, its limited existence is not a problem.

A complete program using 'skiptonextsentence' is given below. This program counts the number of sentences ending with a full stop in a passage of text which finishes with an asterisk after the last full stop.

```
program countsentences (input,output);
var letter:char; count:integer;
procedure skiptonextsentence;
var ch:char;
begin
  repeat
    read(ch)
  until ch = '.'
end;
begin
  count:= 0;
```

```
      repeat
        skiptonextsentence;
        count:= count+1;
        read(letter)
      until letter = '*';
      writeln('no. of sentences = ',count)
   end.
```

Here, it is important to recognise the different uses of the two variables 'letter' and 'ch': 'letter' is both declared and used in the main part of the program whereas 'ch' is used within the procedure and nowhere else.

Though it is usually clearer to choose two different names for the variables in circumstances such as these it is worth noting that no confusion would occur (to the Pascal compiler) if the same name were chosen for both (for example, if we replaced 'letter' throughout by 'ch'). What would happen is that the compiler would recognise two distinct variables of the same name. The one declared in the main program would be made temporarily inaccessible when the procedure was called, only to re-appear on exit with its old value. If this notion is confusing it can always be avoided by choosing different names in the first place!

Note finally that if a **for** loop is used in a procedure then the control variable must be declared as a local variable in ISO Standard Pascal.

7.3   Global variables and parameters

It may well have occurred to readers to question why, in the above example, it is necessary to declare a local variable 'ch' at all, since a perfectly good char variable ('letter') is declared at the top of the program. In fact, subject to the comments above about identifiers of the same name, and control variables, any variable declared at the top of a program is accessible from anywhere in the program, including within procedures, and is for this reason called a *global* variable. Thus, the above program can be re-written by replacing 'ch' by 'letter' and eliminating the local variable declaration from the procedure.

However, making this change to procedure 'skiptonextsentence' is a good example of bad programming practice. There are two main reasons why this is so:

1. 'skiptonextsentence' has lost its independence. Since it now relies on an external declaration of the variable 'letter' it cannot claim to be a logically separate piece of program, neither can it be removed and placed in another program without including 'letter' as a declaration in that other program.

2. In performing a specific task, 'skip to next sentence' has unnecessarily altered the value of a global variable. Though in this program it is reasonably clear that it does not matter that the value of 'letter' is modified by the procedure, the effect in other, perhaps larger, programs may be less obvious and more far-reaching.

Thus, if a variable is required purely locally within a procedure it is always best to declare it as a local variable. More often than not, however, a procedure will be required to take in one or more values from the main program and to return one or more values on completion of a call. This requires some form of communication of values between a program at the time of calling the procedure and the procedure itself. Consider the following example, which uses a procedure to exchange the values in the variables 'x' and 'y'.

```
program exchange (input,output);
var x,y:integer;
procedure xchng;
var temp:integer;
begin
  temp:= x;
  x:= y;
  y:= temp
end;
begin
  .

  .

  .

  xchng;
  .

  .

  .

end.
```

In this program, the exchange sequence within the procedure refers directly to the global variables 'x' and 'y', thus achieving the necessary exchange of values between these variables. Hence, global variables are perhaps the simplest means of communicating values to and from a procedure.

However, once again the notion of a procedure being independent of the main program is violated because 'xchng' will only work in an environment in which 'x' and 'y' have been declared globally. Furthermore, it would be annoyingly inconvenient if later in the same program we wished to exchange the values of two different variables, say 'x' and 'z'. Surely the same procedure could be used for both?

The solution to this problem is to use *parameters* for the two variables whose values are to be exchanged. Parameters have already been used with the standard 'read' and 'write' procedures to enable a value to be input, for example, to any suitably typed variable as in 'read(x)' or 'read(y)'. In a similar way we can redefine the procedure declaration for 'xchng' to accept the two variables as parameters:

```
procedure xchng2 (var first,second:integer);

var temp:integer;

begin
  temp:= first;
  first:= second;
  second:= temp
end;
```

The two parameter variables 'first' and 'second' exist uniquely in the procedure declaration to mark the places that will be filled at a procedure call by the actual variables whose values are to be exchanged. For this reason they are called *formal* or *dummy* parameters. When two variables are to exchange values in the program we write a procedure call which includes the variables as parameters; for example,

```
xchng2(x,y)
```

where 'x' and 'y' are called *actual* parameters.

There must be exactly the same number of actual parameters as formal ones and the correspondence between the two is entirely by position, so that the action on calling the procedure as above is effectively:

> Replace every occurrence of the formal parameter 'first' in the procedure by the actual parameter 'x' and every occurrence of 'second' by 'y' and then obey the resulting statements in the procedure.

On completion of the above call of the procedure the original values of 'x' and 'y' will have been exchanged. We may subsequently call the same procedure with different parameters; for example,

```
xchng2(x,z)
```

and this achieves an exchange of values between the actual parameters in this call, which are 'x' and 'z', assuming that 'z' is added to the integer declarations at the top of the program. The data type of corresponding actual and formal parameters must always be the same. Note that the standard procedures 'read' and 'write' are most unusual in that they allow a variable number and type of actual parameters.

One way of looking at the parameter passing activity in 'xchng2' is to note that 'first' and 'second' are both used to take values (to be exchanged) from the main program into the procedure when it is called and also to take values (that have been exchanged) out of the procedure back into the main program on completion of the procedure statements. We may say that 'first' and 'second' are both input and output parameters of the procedure 'xchng2'.

In many cases, parameters to procedures will not be two-way in the above sense but just input or output. For example, using the **case** statement developed in chapter 6 we may construct a procedure to determine the number of days in a month:

```
procedure daysinmonth (var days,month:integer);
begin
    case month of
            9,4,6,11:days:= 30;
                  2:days:= 28;
     1,3,5,7,8,10,12:days:= 31
    end
end;
```

Once again, 'days' and 'month' are the formal parameters of this procedure declaration for which we shall substitute actual parameters in a call such as:

```
daysinmonth(d,mo)
```

where 'd' and 'mo' have been declared (for example, at the top of the program) as integer variables. Thus, a simple program to print out the number of days in each month of a (non-leap) year is:

```
program printdays (output);
var d,mo:integer;
procedure daysinmonth (var days,month: integer);
```

```
begin
  case month of
          9,4,6,11:days:= 30;
                 2:days:= 28;
    1,3,5,7,8,10,12:days:= 31
  end
end;
begin
  mo:= 1;
  repeat
    daysinmonth(d, mo);
    writeln(d);
    mo:= mo + 1
  until mo > 12
end.
```

In the above example it is clear that, of the two parameters to 'daysinmonth', 'month' is used exclusively as an input parameter and 'days' as an output parameter. This is no more than a statement of the purpose of the procedure: to accept a month number and deliver a number of days as a result.

So far, we have considered only variable parameters; that is, those that are introduced by the word **var** in the procedure heading and which behave as if they are replaced by the actual parameters of a call. However, the fact that 'month' in the above example is used solely to take in a value to the procedure and, hence, is never changed within the procedure (that is, 'month' never occurs on the left-hand side of an assignment statement) means that an alternative approach is possible for this parameter. By changing the way in which the parameters are defined in the procedure heading we can make 'month' into a *value* parameter:

procedure daysinmonth (**var** days:integer; month:integer);

Here, we have removed 'month' from the **var** clause in the parameter list, leaving it defined as being of type integer but not variable. The effective interpretation of parameter passing by value is:

> On entry to the procedure, copy the *value* of the actual parameter into the formal parameter.

Several variables of both **var** and value type may be declared in a procedure heading, according to the syntax of a 'parameter list' (see appendix 1).

Why bother to distinguish two different parameter mechanisms? Apart from making the program slightly more efficient there is one real benefit of value parameters: they allow an expression to be written as the actual parameter. For example, suppose we wish to obtain the number of days in the next month to that held in 'mo' (we assume 'mo' to have a value that is less than 12). If 'mo' is declared as a value parameter we can write

> daysinmonth(d,mo + 1)

Expressions may not be written as actual parameters to non-value procedure parameters.

To prevent possible alteration, ISO-Pascal insists that a **for** loop control variable may be passed *only* as a value parameter to a procedure. It is this restriction which prevents a **for** loop being used in the earlier example above, where 'mo' is passed as a **var** parameter to procedure 'daysinmonth'. In the revised version, where 'mo' is declared as a value parameter it is now possible to use the more obvious '**for** mo: = 1 **to** 12 **do**...' form of loop in place of **repeat-until**.

7.4   Functions

A procedure call is yet another kind of statement in the syntax of Pascal, alongside the assignment statement, **if** statement and so on. A function, on the other hand, such as the standard square root function 'sqrt' occupies a quite different place in the syntax: it is used in expressions. The important distinguishing feature is the single value which is returned as the result of a function call.

New functions can be defined in Pascal in a very similar way to procedures. They begin with the reserved word **function** and may include the same mixture of value and variable parameters as a procedure declaration. In addition to any parameter information, however, the type of function result must be specified in the heading.

The factorial function, '!', for example, is defined as

$$p! = p*(p-1)*(p-2)\ldots*1 \quad (p > 0) \quad \text{For example,}$$
$$= 1 \quad\quad\quad\quad\quad\quad\quad (p = 0) \quad\quad 4! = 4*3*2*1 = 24$$

A Pascal function for factorial is given below:

```
function fact (p:integer):integer;
var i,prod:integer;
begin
  prod: = 1;
  for i: = p downto 1 do prod: = prod*i;
  fact: = prod
end;
```

The function 'fact' takes a single parameter 'p' and delivers a result whose type is stated after a colon following the parameter list. An integer local variable is used as the control variable of a **for** loop ('i') and another ('prod') to accumulate the product of successive numbers from 'p' down to 1 (2 would be sufficient) in forming the factorial.

The last statement in the function shows the manner of assigning the value to be returned as the result of the function. The actual name of the function ('fact') is written on the left-hand side of an assignment statement and given the required factorial value which has been calculated in 'prod'.

Note that 'p' is defined as a value parameter since it is used only to input the value whose factorial is to be determined. This has the advantage over a variable parameter specification in allowing a call that contains an expression as the parameter. We can illustrate a use of 'fact' with a simple program calculating combinations:

The number of ways of choosing 'r' objects from 'n' (written 'nCr') is given by the formula

$$nCr = \frac{n!}{r! \, (n-r)}$$

As an example, given 4 objects designated 'A', 'B', 'C' and 'D', the ways of choosing 2 objects from the 4 are 'AB', 'AC', 'AD', 'BC', 'BD', 'CD' = 6 ways; that is,

$$nCr = \frac{4!}{2! \, (4-2)!} = \frac{4*3*2*1}{2*1*2*1} = \frac{24}{4} = 6$$

If you are so inclined you can use the program to calculate the number of combinations of 8 matches there are in, say, 12 choices on a football pools coupon.

The following program reads values for 'n' and 'r' and prints out 'nCr':

```
program nCrcalc (input,output);
var n,r,ncr:integer;
function fact (p:integer):integer;
var i,prod:integer;
begin
  prod:= 1;
  for i:= p downto 2 do prod:= prod*i;
  fact:= prod
end;
```

```
begin
    read(n,r);
    ncr:= fact(n) div (fact(r)*fact(n-r));
    write('There are',ncr,' ways of choosing',r,' objects from',n)
end.
```

Note that the expression 'n − r' is only acceptable as an actual parameter of 'fact' because 'p' is a value parameter. Finally, one has to be a little careful when using 'fact' in its present form since the factorial of even quite small numbers is very large (11! is nearly 40 million). If there is any danger of exceeding the maximum size of an integer value on your computer it will be necessary to change the type of result of the function and its local variable 'prod' to 'real' to give a much larger range, and to do the arithmetic using reals.

The choice between using a procedure or a function is a matter of programmer convenience. If a routine generates only a single result which can be put to use directly in an expression then the preference for a function is clear and strong. Note, finally, that the procedure 'daysinmonth' is a candidate for being re-written as a function in many applications.

Exercises

7.1 Write a 'logoprint' procedure using your own design.

7.2 Using the procedure heading

procedure countsp (**var** spcount:integer);

write a program to count spaces on a line based on program 'countspaces' in chapter 6 but using a procedure to do the counting and to return the count in the parameter 'spcount'.

7.3 As part of a program to average practical marks it is required to convert grades from the six point letter format (A, B+, B−, C, D, E) into a corresponding numerical scale (1, 2, 3, 4, 5, 6). Complete a procedure to perform this conversion whose heading and parameter specifications are

procedure convertgrades (gradeletter, gradequalifier:char; **var** mark:integer);

where, on calling the procedure,

'gradeletter' holds the main letter grade ('A', 'B', 'C', 'D', or 'E'),

'gradequalifier' holds '+' or '−' if 'gradeletter' = 'B'
   and is undefined otherwise;
the corresponding numerical grade (1–6) is returned in 'mark'.

7.4 Write a Pascal function that takes two integer parameters 'x' and 'y', determines if 'x' is a multiple of 'y' and returns the Boolean result of this test.

7.5 Write a Pascal function that will take in a unit of time expressed in hours, minutes and seconds (three integer parameters) and deliver as an integer result the corresponding length of time in seconds. Check that your parameters are of the most appropriate type (**var** or value).

Input and output

No other area of programming seems to have presented the designers of programming languages with as many headaches as the mechanisms for moving values of data into and out of programs. Indeed, some of the most rigorous language definitions have stopped short of giving more than passing hints about how input and output should be implemented at all, and this has led to incompatibilities between implementations of the same programming language on different computers. The difficulties stem from the fact that, ultimately, the task of communicating data to and from the user is not the responsibility of the programming language system but of the environment in which that system resides: that is, the 'operating system' of the computer. Unfortunately, each different computer tends to have a different operating system and, for reasons which are presumably apparent to their creators, there is no guarantee of a universally compatible set of input/output facilities. In all fairness to the writers of operating systems, differences between implementations are also brought about by enthusiastic language implementers adding extra, or even totally novel, procedures. Pascal has not entirely escaped this confusing practice though, fortunately, the level of agreement is encouragingly high.

The relevance of all this to the programmer is that it is difficult to talk authoritatively about some aspects of input and output in a general book on programming when it is probable that local variations will apply. Certainly, all of the facilities introduced in this chapter will be available in all standard Pascal implementations. Points at which local documentation should be consulted are marked later in the book.

8.1 Modes of programming

In recent years there has been a quite rapid drift away from punched card and paper tape as means of program and data input to computers in favour of interactive terminals, notably visual display units (VDUs). The VDU offers fast, convenient input and output for many kinds of computer interaction. Modes of programming have changed as a direct result – *batch* processing, in which programs are packed end-to-end and processed as a composite batch, usually of punched cards, has been largely replaced by *conversational* mode programming with direct terminal–computer dialogue. The variety of available printing devices has grown, though increased use of screen displays for transient program and data listing considerably reduces the need to generate 'hard-copy' output and should leave trees to be put to a better use in the future.

A VDU is actually two devices in one: an input keyboard and an output screen display which work independently. Since it is helpful to be able to see which keys have been typed it is usual for the computer to 'echo' any keyboard characters it receives back to the VDU screen except when typing, for example, a secret password.

Initial program entry and subsequent editing are particularly well-suited to the VDU with its fast action and correcting facilities as opposed to rather tedious repunching of cards or tape in an older batch system. However, the net result of both approaches is the same, and we should, perhaps, beware of rushing onto an interactive computer terminal too quickly. In particular, there are few programmers able to 'compose' good programs for even simple tasks directly at a computer keyboard. Until an equivalent electronic device is available, the pencil and paper are still the most useful first tools.

All of these input/output devices ('peripherals') have one important characteristic in common: they are all character-based. In other words, all communication between peripherals such as VDUs, card readers, printers, etc. and the computer itself takes place in the form of sequences of characters in the character set of the computer. This is important to the design of input and output facilities in Pascal because it allows a consistent approach to be developed regardless of the physical nature of the peripheral device attached to the computer.

All Pascal programs have available to them a standard input channel or 'stream' called *input* and a standard output 'stream' called *output*, both of which are organised entirely in terms of lines of characters. The terminology stems from the idea of characters 'flowing' one after the other from peripheral to computer or vice versa. A program may read values from the input stream or write characters out onto the output stream using procedures that require no insight into the physical nature of the peripheral at the other end. It is a major function of the operating system of the computer to provide any necessary transformations between a generalised I/O scheme of this nature and the actual peripherals concerned and to allow flexible reassignment of peripherals. An example of this latter would be to allow a simple change in an operating system command to send output from a Pascal program to a printer instead of to a VDU screen, without in any way needing to change the Pascal program itself.

Many of the differences between Pascal systems arise because of the need to send data to and from *non* text-based peripherals such as graphics terminals which allow pictures to be drawn on a screen as opposed to just characters. Usually, a set of additional standard procedures will form the core of language extensions to permit non text-based I/O but the precise method of using these peripherals must be studied from local documentation.

The foregoing remarks explain the reason for including the words 'input' and/or 'output' in brackets after the program name when these streams are to be used (though some Pascal implementations have abandoned this requirement). A more advanced treatment of input and output in terms of *files* is given in chapter 12.

8.2　Read and readln

These two procedures are used to take in values from the standard input stream and assign them to variables; for example,

　　　read(a,b,c)

As mentioned earlier, these input procedures and the ones for output which are described later are unusual since a variable number of parameters of different types is permitted. Values are assigned to the variables in left-to-right order, that is, first 'a', then 'b', then 'c' in the above example. The way in which characters arriving in the input stream are interpreted depends on the data type of the variable as follows:

(*a*) *integer and real*. Decimal numbers are expected in the format appropriate for Pascal integer or real numbers as defined in the syntax diagrams. They may be preceded by an optional sign. For integers this means sequences of digits such as

　　　1234
　　　−65
　　　+5555

and they must be free of embellishments such as commas or internal spaces. For reals, the range of possibilities is rather greater: an optional sign followed by a number in the syntax shown in figure 8.1.

Examples are

    1234
    3.14159
    − 329.0
    + 529.72
    5.2972E + 2

The last of these numbers is in 'floating-point' format, commonly called 'scientific notation'. It is a representation of the method of writing a number as a value times a power of ten, as in

$$5.2972 \times 10^2$$

where '5.2972' is called the 'mantissa' and '2' is the exponent denoted by 'E' in the input syntax. Hence, the last two examples in the above list represent the same value.

Note that, for convenience, an integer value is accepted for input to a real variable.

One further problem is the recognition of the start and finish of a number and this is done as follows. Any number of spaces and newlines will be skipped over automatically in the input stream to find the start of a new number. Subsequent characters are taken as part of that number until a character is found which cannot be part of the number (for example, a space). Thus, successive numbers must be separated by at least one space or newline.

(*b*) *char*. Reading a value into a char variable means literally taking the next character in the input stream as this value, with no automatic skipping of spaces or new lines. Three cases deserve special mention:

Figure 8.1. Unsigned number.

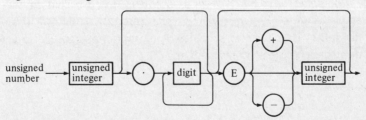

1. When the last character on a line is read the standard Boolean function 'eoln' (end of line) is set 'true' and this provides a convenient way for the programmer to test for the end of a line.
2. The next character to be read when 'eoln' is 'true' is a specially inserted 'end of line' character which is in fact a space. The character after this one is the first on the next line of input.
3. In some programs it is desirable to know when the input stream is completely exhausted; for example, when data are taken from a source other than a terminal keyboard. A Boolean function 'eof' (end of file) is set to 'true' when the last character in the file has been read.

Note that when reading either numbers or characters it is not possible to go back through the data at any stage, which means that a number, for example, may only be read once.

'Readln' may be called without parameters at all:

readln

The effect is to skip over any remaining items on the current line in the input stream, setting the next read position at the beginning of the following line. The meaning of 'readln(a,b,c)' is exactly the same as

read(a,b,c);
readln

Direct input of Boolean values is not permitted.

Note finally that a common mistake made by beginners is to type in more than the actual data values themselves in response to a read statement. With three integer variables in a read statement 'read(a,b,c)', for example, *only* three integers are expected, as in

10   253   −12

and relationships to the variable names themselves must certainly *not* be added as in

a = 10   b = 253   c = −12

8.3   Write and writeln

A write statement is used to send characters out on the standard output stream and has the general form

write(output list)

where an output list consists of one or more output values separated by commas. Each item in the list must give a value which is either integer, real, Boolean, char, or a string of characters enclosed in single quotes. In many cases the items will be single variable identifiers but any integer or real expression is permitted; for example,

```
write(4.25/3.66)
write(a,b,c/2)
write('The answer is',a)
```

Note that although a Boolean value cannot be input directly it may be printed using 'write'. The word 'True' or 'False' is written onto the output stream.

An important consideration in using 'write' to output values is the number of character positions occupied by each value in the output stream and, ultimately, on the screen or printed page. In many applications it may be fitting to modify the printing format of tabulated numbers, for example, to make them aligned for neatness and ease of reading. Further means of control over the printing of real numbers to an appropriate precision is an equally desirable facility.

To illustrate the exercise of control over printing formats consider the write statement

```
write('hello',145,'p is',1.45,' pounds')
```

Output from this statement as it stands will be similar to

```
hello       145p is 1.4499998092651e+00 pounds
```

Note here that characters in strings (enclosed in quotes) are output in exactly the format they are written but a number of spaces have been inserted in the printing of both the integer and real numbers. This is because every value in the output list of a write statement has an associated *field-width* which denotes the number of character positions it will occupy in the output stream. The field-widths of integer and real values depend on the Pascal implementation, though that of a char value will certainly be 1. The field-width setting is usually chosen to permit output of the largest integer or real number in that implementation and filled out from the left with spaces for smaller values.

Regardless of the implementation, the field-width can be altered by following the value to be printed with a colon and a new field-width. For example, given an integer 'count' whose value is 132, the statement

```
write(count:4)
```

will output the value 132 right-specified in 4 print positions, that is, as

_132   (_represents a space)

In general, a field-width can be specified as any expression delivering a positive integer value greater than or equal to 1. If a number is too large to fit into a given width then the layout will be spoilt by using extra print positions without corrupting the value by truncation.

A more obvious clumsiness of the output from the earlier write statement is the printing of the real value by default in floating-point format. This is quite out of place in this particular example where a value of pounds and hundredths of pounds is anticipated. The field-width can be varied as in the integer case but this does not solve the problem. The answer is to specify both a field-width and a *fraction-length*, that is, the number of digits that are to follow the decimal point, as in

pi: = 3.14159;   {'pi' real}
write(pi:5:2)

which results in the value

_3.14

being printed. Note that a field-width specified for a real number must leave room for at least one leading space. Values are rounded to the number of places of decimals stated in the fraction-length (equal to 2 in the above example). As a further example,

write(pi:7:3)

gives

_ _ 3.142

Here, finally, is an improved version of the earlier write statement:

write('hello',145:4,'p is',1.45:6:2,' pounds')

which gives

hello 145p is   1.45 pounds

Note that 'writeln(a,b,c)' is exactly equivalent to

write(a,b,c);
writeln

and results in a new line being taken *after* the values have been printed.

Exercises

8.1 Construct a write statement to output a date held in three integer variables 'day', 'month' and 'year' in the format suggested by the example '21/8/1982'.

8.2 Show how a loop may be written to read dates in the above format, each on a separate line, ending with a date whose day is marked as zero. Write out each date in the format '21–8–1982' after reading it in.

8.3 Write a program that will print a diagonal line of asterisks on the VDU screen or printer, starting in the top left-hand corner. (Hint: the field-width of a character output may be variable.)

8.4 Write a program to tabulate integers and their squares and cubes for values between two limits read in as data. Include a suitable 'prompt' for the input and place the headings 'number', 'square' and 'cube' above the appropriate columns.

8.5 Write a program to send out an 'SOS' call on the 'bell' of the computer terminal if this feature is available (three short bleeps followed by three long and three more short).

Note: in ASCII, the 'bell' character has a code of 7 and may be output using 'write(chr(7))'. You will need to use some 'dummy' **for** statements to introduce delays between the bleeps.

Part 2

Problem solving by computer

Program design

Truth lies within a little and certain compass, but error is immense.
Reflections upon Exile, Henry St. John, Viscount Bolingbroke
(1678–1751)

In chapter 3 we looked at the process of taking a problem and devising an algorithm as a suitable base for a computer program. We noted that the derivation of the basic algorithm is a task that is difficult to describe in abstract terms but that it is a skill that one acquires primarily by experience. In this chapter we underline the continuous nature of program development, from problem to program, developing a framework for program design that may be useful to us in solving any problem.

Programs of the kind we have met so far have in common that by computing standards they are all short. Each contains less than a page of coding and each represents a solution to a problem that is immediately 'tenable' in the sense that we can visualise a complete solution to a limited problem. In the 'real world', computer programs rarely fall into this category. A computer program to control a nuclear reactor in a power station, for instance, would represent the efforts of many programmers for many hours or even years (frequently measured literally in units of man-hours or man-years). Experience has shown that it is a recipe for disaster to attempt to program a task of this magnitude, or even substantially smaller ones, by the direct approach we adopted in writing these small programs.

A key word here is *structure*, and our aim should be to write *structured programs*.

9.1   'Good' programs

In a general sense a very reasonable goal in problem solving would seem to be to write 'good' computer programs to perform specified tasks. What do we mean by 'good' in this context?

For certain tasks, desirable features of a program will be measured in terms of machine efficiency: does the program execute rapidly or does it occupy a minimum number of storage locations, for example? In the days when computer hardware was expensive and stores relatively small, such considerations were paramount. After all, the most elegant program is of no use if it will not fit into your computer! However, simple machine efficiency is by no means the only measure of a 'good' program and this is particularly true today as the power of computers increases and as the relative cost of hardware falls. The dominant cost in developing most complete computer systems has drifted from raw hardware expense to the cost of software. A professional computer programmer's time is an expensive commodity and this obliges us to include programming time and effort in our efficiency calculation. Since most large systems are the product of more than one programmer, a 'good' program may be deemed to be one that is easily understood by another programmer or that can be combined with other programs easily and predictably.

Most importantly, a 'good' program should be a correct program. This may seem obvious but in fact it is rare that a program is known to be completely free of errors. Errors residing in a program are referred to by the charming title of *bugs* and 'debugging' a program can occupy a disproportionate length of time. A program does not have to be very long for there to be so many possible logic paths that it becomes impossible to check each one individually. Quite often bugs lie dormant in a program for a long time, only to spring to life when an unusual combination of input data are entered, for example. It is this, more than anything else, that gives us incentive to develop and use a structured approach to the design of all our programs, from the smallest up.

9.2   Structured programs

Structured programming is the term used to cover a whole spectrum of disciplined approaches to the design and implementation of programs. Some of the ideas, such as the division of large programming tasks into smaller units tackled by separate programmers with precisely defined interfaces between them, have entire books dedicated to detailed techniques. At a more basic level, however, we can identify three areas that are relevant to writing even quite small programs:

1. The size of program units.
2. Hierarchy.
3. Control structures.

Informally, we should be wary of trying to do too much programming at once. The size of any section of a program should be limited to that which may be safely tackled 'in one go'. The earlier programs in part 1 are examples of such manageable units. A primary aim of the program design technique outlined later is to divide any problem that is larger than this into smaller, self-contained units which may be tackled separately and then combined into one program.

Tied in with this approach is the notion of hierarchical structure in problem solving. We can illustrate this with a simple non-computing problem. At the highest level, an algorithm to describe the construction of a garden pond is brief but unhelpful:

   build pond

At a slightly greater level of detail we expand the task into, perhaps, three sub-tasks:

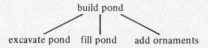

Similarly, each of these sub-problems may be expanded into further, simpler tasks where necessary, to construct a hierarchical structure representing the overall task of building a pond:

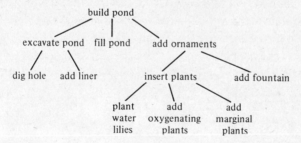

Eventually, a stage will be reached where the level of description is adequate for a particular task without further refinement ('adequate', here, may mean that the set of instructions could be given to someone to carry out directly, for example). The sub-tasks, combined under hierarchical control form a complete and detailed description of a solution to the overall problem. Applied to programming, this technique of refining a problem into progressively simpler tasks is known as 'top-down program development'.

Control structures play an important part in program design. In particular, the flow of control from statement to statement should be restricted so that there is only one point of entry to a construction (for example, a block, conditional statement or loop) and one exit. This is easy to achieve in Pascal since the language was designed to provide suitable control structures, two of which are outlined in figure 9.1.

Difficulties arise when control may be transferred arbitrarily about a program, thus bypassing the hierarchical structure. Keen readers may have noticed a statement defined in the syntax diagrams in appendix 1 called 'goto'. Its effect is beautifully simple: by defining a label which may be attached to a statement elsewhere in the program we may jump directly to this statement from almost anywhere using **goto**. In fact, several other programming languages rely on **goto** as the only way to construct conditional and even repetition structures. Powerful as it is, however, there is nothing more difficult to follow than a program containing a large number of **goto**s and experience has shown that this one statement is responsible for more programming errors than almost any other. One of the reasons for this is that program statements that are relevant to a specific sub-task may be spread out in different places in the program and linked by **goto**s. They are, hence, more difficult to understand and to manage than if all such statements were grouped together in one place by using the appropriate control structure.

In short, the conclusion is to avoid the use of **goto** wherever possible. There are very few occasions indeed when the use of **goto** improves a Pascal program and there are better constructions available in the Pascal programmer's armoury.

Figure 9.1. Examples of control structures.

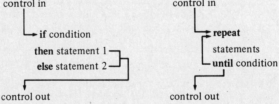

9.3 Comments

One aid to making programs more readable is to insert short comments in the text for the reader's benefit. In Pascal, comments are surrounded by curly brackets (or by (* and *)). They may be inserted at any place in the program where a space would be permitted. A comment may be used, for example, to explain the meaning of a section of coding that may not be totally self evident, or to label the beginning or end of a compound structure. Comments are ignored by the compiler (technically they are equivalent to a space). Some examples of their use are given below.

Example 1	*Example 2*
{exchange first & last values}	**begin**
begin	**case** day **of**
temp:= first;	2,3,4,5,6 :action1; {weekday}
first:= last;	1,7 :action2 {weekend}
last:= temp	**end** {of **case**}
end	**end**

It is worth remembering, however, that Pascal was designed to encourage the 'self-documenting' of programs. Careful choice of identifiers and a well thought out layout make the need for copious comments quite redundant.

9.4 Data structure

Programming is made much easier, more reliable and programs more straightforward to understand if the right data structure is chosen for the right task. At the most basic level this implies using an integer in circumstances where an integer is clearly demanded, avoiding any temptation to use a real variable instead. More seriously, as mentioned in chapter 2, it is still necessary in some current programming languages to represent characters by integers (1 for an 'A', 2 for a 'B', etc.). This practice is not only inelegant it is tedious and error prone. The greatest improvement in the design of modern programming languages has been the provision of flexible data structuring facilities and we shall try to emphasise these in later examples.

One Pascal feature which has not been mentioned so far and which is intended to help in program design is the 'const' facility: **const** declarations may be made before **var** declarations in a program to introduce identifiers of constant data values. For example, if we intend to read in characters and test to see if a full stop is read we may declare

    const fullstop = '.';

before the **var** declarations at the head of the program (or procedure in which the constant identifier is to be used). We may then use 'fullstop' in any position where the char constant '.' would be appropriate; for example,

> **if** ch = fullstop
>   **then** ...

(where 'ch' is a char variable).

Constant identifiers for values of any of the standard data types may be introduced, as we shall see in later chapters. For the moment, note that a **const** declaration is similar in syntax to a **var** declaration (see the syntax diagrams in appendix 1) in that the word **const** appears just once, but several constants may be introduced, each separated from the last by a semicolon, as in

> **const**   colon = ':';
>   vatrate = 15;
>   pi = 3.14159;

Unlike **var** declarations, however, the name of the data type of each introduced identifier is not required. The Pascal compiler can work out for itself the data type by examining the structure of the constant value.

Finally, note again that **const**s, if there are any, will always be the first declarations following a program or procedure heading.

9.5   Top-down program design – a case study

Top-down design is a technique for refining a problem solution into progressively more detailed steps until a program emerges in a natural, continuous manner. It relies more on common sense and experience than on formal rules and the following example is used to introduce basic ideas which will be developed further in later programs. We begin with a specification of the problem in English:

> Calculate and print the minimum number and denominations of coins (50p, 10p, 5p, 2p, 1p) required to make up change to a value that is less than £1.

We shall select a brief title to represent this as our *top-level description* of the problem:

> Find and print change

The next step is to apply a 'divide and rule' philosophy to this initial description, dividing the task into at least two smaller sub-tasks as in:

> read changevalue
> calculate and print change

This does not give us startling insight into solving the problem but the principle is sound. As long as we can continue to divide steps into two or more simpler ones we must eventually win. In particular, the first of these steps, 'read changevalue' is already one that is sufficiently manageable to tackle directly and we can ignore it for the time being. Turning to the second step we may refine this into further sub-tasks:

> Set highest denomination (50p)
>
> **while** there is still change to be given **do**
>   **begin**
>   calculate number of coins of this denomination
>   calculate change still to be given
>   write number of coins (if any)
>   set next denomination
>   **end**

This is the most important stage in the design process for this example. We have recognised a pattern in the problem: that we may deal with each denomination of coinage in a similar way, starting with the 50p pieces and attempting to use as many of these as possible before going on to the next denomination. A loop has emerged, expressed in some of the syntax of Pascal liberally mixed with less precise statements in English.

It is important to recognise that there is nothing absolute about this last step. Different programmers will provide different and often equally acceptable divisions of the same problem (doubtless there is a better solution than the one above). Indeed, it is rare for two programmers to generate exactly the same solution to a given problem and you should not be discouraged if this particular solution did not immediately spring into your mind. In addition, we must certainly be prepared at any stage to decide that we are on the wrong track and to go back to an earlier stage to try alternative approaches.

In arriving at the step described above we now have an increasingly clear idea of some of the data structures that will be used in the eventual program. It is good practice at this stage to define the most important of these, particularly if the nature of some of the structures is quite complex.

In this case the data structures are straightforward. We require several integer variables, notably

> changevalue . . the number of pence to be returned as change
> coinvalue. . . . the denomination of coinage being considered (50, 10, 5, 2 or 1)
> noofcoins. . . . to count the number of coins of one denomination

To set 'coinvalue' successively to 50, 10, etc. we shall use a **case** statement with an integer selector 'coinno' which is initialised to 1 and incremented by 1 after each denomination has been considered, giving a new refinement of the last level of the description:

```
coinno: = 1;
while changevalue > 0 do
  begin
    {Determine coin value}
    case coinno of
      1:coinvalue: = 50;
      2:coinvalue: = 10;
      3:coinvalue: = 5;
      4:coinvalue: = 2;
      5:coinvalue: = 1
    end;

    calculate noofcoins of this denomination
    calculate change still to be given
    write number of coins (if any)
    coinno: = coinno + 1
  end {of loop for one denomination}
```

The final refinement before a complete program is attempted must be directed at the heart of the program – 'calculate noofcoins of this denomination'. It is not uncommon to write such central coding as the last step in the program design. We can use **div** to provide the integer number of coins of the set denomination and **mod** to calculate the change remaining.

```
noofcoins: = changevalue div coinvalue;
changevalue: = changevalue mod coinvalue
```

Finally, we put all the pieces together into a complete program, adding a heading and all declarations:

```
program changegiver(input,output);
var changevalue, coinvalue, noofcoins, coinno:integer;
begin
   read(changevalue);
   coinno:= 1;
   while changevalue > 0 do
      begin
         case coinno of
            1:coinvalue:= 50;
            2:coinvalue:= 10;
            3:coinvalue:= 5;
            4:coinvalue:= 2;
            5:coinvalue:= 1
         end;
         noofcoins:= changevalue div coinvalue;
         changevalue:= changevalue mod coinvalue;
         if noofcoins > 0
            then writeln(noofcoins:2,' x ',coinvalue:2,'p');
         coinno:= coinno+1
      end
end.
```

Typical output from this program is shown below for a value of 78 entered as the 'changevalue':

```
1 x 50p
2 x 10p
1 x 5p
1 x 2p
1 x 1p
```

A general criticism of the above program is the lack of a suitable 'prompt' to the user for input if the program is to be used in an interactive environment. Here, we could include the prompt

write('Enter change:');

immediately before the read statement to leave the user in no doubt as to what is expected next.

'Changegiver' is a problem requiring relatively few items of data where the emphasis is concentrated on developing the algorithm. In general, the amount of data manipulated in a program provides a convenient way of dividing programs into categories. In some programs, for example, all the data relevant to the problem can be held in variables within the program. 'Changegiver' is an example of such a program. With larger amounts of data, however, a different technique of storing data may be required and with still larger 'files' of data to process it may only be possible to hold a small portion of the data within the program at any one time. We shall look at some examples of programs in each of these categories in subsequent chapters.

Exercises

9.1 Modify the program 'changegiver' to include 20p coins in the change.

9.2 Design an algorithm and write a program to read in a digit and an integer number and to print out whether that digit is present in the number. (Hint: use **div** and **mod**.)

9.3 Design an algorithm and a program to read today's date (as, for example, '21/8/82') and print out tomorrow's date.

Problems involving small quantities of data

In some applications, the writing of an algorithm to solve a problem dominates the programming task, with the data and subsequent data structures tending to be relatively simple. Here, we shall concentrate on examples of programs in this category and in doing so we shall use many of the basic programming structures introduced in earlier chapters.

10.1   A simple program

The first example below illustrates a common requirement, to produce a table of results based on different values of a variable – in this case, a table of conversions from miles per gallon to kilometres per litre.

Example 10.1

Print a chart showing conversions to kilometres per litre for values of miles per gallon from 10 to 60.

As a first refinement, we recognise the repetitive nature of this task in

for mpg: = lowmpg **to** highmpg **do**
   begin
      convert mpg to kpl
      print mpg and kpl
   end

The use of 'lowmpg' and 'highmpg' reflects our desire to generalise the program. If, as in this case, the values are to be fixed, we may include these two identifiers in a **const** declaration at the head of the program as suggested in section 9.4. The constant factor for converting from miles per gallon to kilometres per litre is a further candidate for **const** treatment. The rest of the program is relatively straightforward and we may feel sufficiently confident at this point to progress to a complete program from the outline algorithm above:

```
program mpgtokpl (output);
const  lowmpg = 10;
       highmpg = 60;
       conversionfactor = 0.354;
var  mpg:integer;
     kpl:real;
begin
   writeln('MPG    KPL');   {a heading for the table}
   for mpg: = lowmpg to highmpg do
     begin
       kpl: = mpg*conversionfactor;
       writeln(mpg:3,'    ',kpl:6:2)
     end
end.
```

Note, here, that the expression performing the conversion contains a mixture of integer and real operands and delivers a real result in accordance with the rules of operators. The resulting 'kilometres per litre' value is output with a field-width of 6 and precision of 2 decimal places. Although this precision was selected arbitrarily, note that it would be wrong to print out the value to any greater precision without increasing the precision of the conversion factor. The output from this program is outlined below:

MPG	KPL
10	3.54
11	3.89
12	4.25
.	.
.	.
.	.
60	21.24

To make this program more generally applicable we may prefer to read in the limits for conversion to miles per gallon. In addition, it may be desirable to print the conversion at intervals other than 1, but note that a complete change of loop structure is needed to cope with an arbitrary interval:

```
program anympgtokpl (input,output);
const conversionfactor = 0.354;
var  mpg,lowmpg,highmpg,interval:integer;
     kpl:real;
begin
   write('Enter low, high and interval values:');
   read(lowmpg,highmpg,interval);
   writeln('MPG     KPL');

   mpg: = lowmpg;
   while mpg < = highmpg do
     begin
        kpl: = mpg*conversionfactor;
        writeln(mpg:3,'    ',kpl:6:2);
        mpg: = mpg+interval
     end
end.
```

10.2   Conditionals in use

Many programs involve testing one variable against several values, selecting different calculations depending on the result of the comparison. Although we may always do the comparison using nested **if** constructions, the **case** statement was designed specifically for this purpose. Both approaches are illustrated in the next example.

Example 10.2

Convert Roman numerals containing the symbols L, X, V and I to Arabic form.

Normally, the equivalent Arabic values of the Roman numerals L, X, V and I are 50, 10, 5 and 1, respectively. In some circumstances, however, a Roman numeral is used to indicate a deduction from the following character value, as shown in the following examples:

Roman	Arabic
I	1
II	2
III	3
IV	4
V	5
IX	9
XL	40

Thus, our algorithm must examine each Roman numeral in turn (read as a character), taking into account, where necessary, the numeral that follows, to determine the equivalent Arabic number. Firstly, to be consistent with our policy of avoiding too many literals we declare some constants to represent the numerals:

```
const  L = 'L';
       X = 'X';
       V = 'V';
       I = 'I';
       space = ' ';
```

Recognising the need to 'look ahead' by one character we may elaborate the program design to:

```
read first romanchar
repeat
    read followingchar
    calculate and accumulate the Arabic value of romanchar
    romanchar: = followingchar
until followingchar = space
write Arabic value
```

A single space is assumed to mark the end of the Roman number. The rules for calculating the corresponding Arabic value of a numeral can be expressed as a series of tests and actions in a nested **if**:

```
if romanchar = L
  then arabicvalue: = 50
  else if romanchar = X
        then if followingchar = L
               then arabicvalue: = −10
               else arabicvalue: = 10
        else if romanchar = V
              then arabicvalue: = 5
              else if romanchar = I
                    then if (followingchar = V) or
                            (followingchar = X)
                          then arabicvalue: = −1
                          else arabicvalue: = 1
```

noting the pattern of indentation which ensures visual matching of the correct **else** with its preceding **then**.

This construction is valid but clumsy and we have met a better one. Since most of the tests are performed on the same variable (romanchar), we may use a **case** statement instead of the nested **if**s:

```
case romanchar of
    L: arabicvalue:= 50;
    X: if followingchar = L
        then arabicvalue:= -10
        else arabicvalue:= 10;
    V: arabicvalue:= 5;
    I: if (followingchar = V) or (followingchar = X)
        then arabicvalue:= -1
        else arabicvalue:= 1
end
```

The data structures required in this program are once again very simple. As well as the two character variables 'romanchar' and 'followingchar' we shall introduce an integer variable 'arabicno' to accumulate the sum of the individual 'arabicvalue' integers in the final program:

```
program romantoarabic (input,output);
const  L = 'L';X = 'X';V = 'V';I = 'I';
       space = ' ';
var  romanchar,followingchar:char;
     arabicno,arabicvalue:integer;
begin
  arabicno:= 0;
  read(romanchar);
  repeat
    read(followingchar);
    case romanchar of
        L: arabicvalue:= 50;
        X: if followingchar = L
            then arabicvalue:= -10
            else arabicvalue:= 10;
        V: arabicvalue:= 5;
        I: if (followingchar = V) or (followingchar = X)
            then arabicvalue:= -1
            else arabicvalue:= 1
    end;
```

```
        arabicno: = arabicno + arabicvalue;
        romanchar: = followingchar
   until followingchar = space;
   write(arabicno)
end.
```

In practice, this program would need tightening up considerably. There are two particularly serious sources of potential error:

1. The program as it stands performs no checks on the Roman numerals that are entered. Thus, a nonsense character string such as 'IIX' will be accepted and the result '10' output without comment. Similarly, characters other than 'L', 'X', 'V' and 'I' will be accepted, even though there is no '**case**' entry for such characters. This will lead to a run-time error without a sensible error message for the user. It would be wise to check the incoming characters for both the above faults, printing out meaningful messages accordingly.
2. For a similar reason to the above, the program will fail if it is supplied with just spaces. Since there is no Roman numeral for zero we may wish a space on its own to indicate a value of zero. Once again, there is no choice in the **case** statement for a space. Perhaps the neatest solution to this problem would be to substitute a **while** statement for the '**repeat–until**' so that the test for a space as the end of a number is performed before the **case** statement is entered.

On a more general point, the modifications required to perform the above checking, especially those concerned with verifying the syntax of incoming numerals, would more than double the length of this program. We must expect, therefore, to divert considerable attention in this direction in many applications. In particular, comprehensive checking of input data and sometimes of data values as they are calculated in a program is an important way of reducing the likelihood of ridiculous results being generated. There really is no excuse, for example, for a company to allow negative or grossly overcharged bills to be issued to customers when relatively simple checking of data in the relevant programs should warn of likely mistakes in entering the original data.

10.3   Looping the loop

Inside a **for** statement, the control variable is available for use if required, as we saw in the first miles per gallon to kilometres per litre conversion program. The structure of a **for** statement may be represented as

> **for** var1 := start1 **to** finish1 **do**
>   statement using var1 in expressions

remembering that the statement may be a compound statement. In other words, we may repeat a statement for different values of a single variable.

On occasion, we need to repeat a statement for combinations of values of more than one variable and we achieve this by 'nesting' one or more loops within an outer loop as shown below:

> outer { **for** var1 := start1 **to** finish1 **do**
> loop { inner { **for** var2 := start2 **to** finish2 **do**
>   loop { statement using var1 and var2 in expressions

Here, the repetitions of the inner **for** statement are completed for *each* value of 'var1' set by the outer loop. We may illustrate this process with a simple example.

> *Example 10.3*
> Generate and print out the 2 times to 12 times multiplication tables.

This is not a very useful program but the example will serve to illustrate the basic principles. We will arrange for the output of this program to look like the following:

$$2 \times 1 = \qquad 2$$
$$2 \times 2 = \qquad 4$$
$$\cdot$$
$$\cdot$$
$$\cdot$$
$$2 \times 12 = \qquad 24$$
$$3 \times 1 = \qquad 3$$
$$\cdot$$
$$\cdot$$
$$\cdot$$
$$12 \times 12 = \qquad 144$$

This is clearly a repetitive task, with 12 entries in each of 11 tables to calculate. Firstly, recognising the similarity between each table ($2\times$, $3\times$, $4\times$, etc.) we can assert

> **for** tablenumber: = 2 **to** 12 **do**
>   generate the multiplication table for this value of 'tablenumber'

Within each table we have a further repetitive process to print the entries:

> **for** multiplier: = 1 **to** 12 **do**
>   write one table line

The 'one table line' to be written out is determined from the values of 'tablenumber' and 'multiplier' as shown in the surprisingly short complete program below:

```
program timestables (output);
var tablenumber, multiplier: integer;
begin
  for tablenumber: = 2 to 12 do
    for multiplier: = 1 to 12 do
      writeln(tablenumber:2,' x ',multiplier:2,' = ',
              (tablenumber*multiplier):6)
end.
```

Let us look more closely at the operation of these nested loops:

> **for** tablenumber: = 2 **to** 12 **do**
>   **for** multiplier: = 1 **to** 12 **do**
>
> statement 1
>
>   writeln(...)   statement 2

Statement 1 is executed 11 times; statement 2, 12 times within each execution of statement 1. Thus, the 'writeln' statement is executed a total of $11 \times 12 = 132$ times with values of 'tablenumber' and 'multiplier' of $(2,1)$, $(2,2)$, ... $(2,12)$, $(3,1)$, etc. up to $(12,12)$.

10.4   Alternative strategies

As an example of a problem that may be approached in two radically different ways consider the following puzzle.

Example 10.4

Find all the numbers less than 1000 for which the sum of the cubes of the digits of the number is equal to the number itself. For example,

$$153 = 1^3 + 5^3 + 3^3$$

One approach, which we may term the 'analysis' technique is based on an initial problem breakdown of

```
begin
    for number: = 0 to 999 do
        check number and print it out if sum of cubes = number
end
```

For any number we need to extract the constituent digits, and the now familiar **div** operator will do this. If the three digits are declared as integers 'd1', 'd2' and 'd3', then

```
d1: = number div 100;          {the hundreds digit}
d2: = (number − d1*100) div 10;   {the tens digit}
d3: = number − (d1*100 + d2*10);  {the units digit}
```

The test and output is straightforward and a complete program is given below.

```
program cubes (output);
var number, d1, d2, d3: integer;
begin
  for number: = 0 to 999 do
    begin
      d1: = number div 100;
      d2: = (number − d1*100) div 10;
      d3: = number − (d1*100 + d2*10);
      if d1*d1*d1 + d2*d2*d2 + d3*d3*d3 = number
        then write(number)
    end
end.
```

Suppose that we reverse our approach to the problem. Instead of starting with the number and breaking it down into constituent digits we begin by taking three values for 'd1', 'd2' and 'd3' and generate the number from these. We may call this the 'synthesis' technique.

Generating the numbers is easy:

number:= d1*100+d2*10+d3

To repeat for all numbers up to 1000 requires a set of nested loops to generate all combinations of 0 to 9 for each digit:

```
for d1:= 0 to 9 do
  for d2:= 0 to 9 do
    for d3:= 0 to 9 do
      begin
        number:= d1*100+d2*10+d3;
        if d1*d1*d1+d2*d2*d2+d3*d3*d3 = number
        then write(number)
      end
```

Rather like the drums on a fruit machine the digits d1, d2 and d3 are varied by the loop so that within the compound statement they assume successive values:

d1	d2	d3
0	0	0
0	0	1
0	0	2
	.	
	.	
	.	
0	0	9
0	1	0
0	1	1
	.	
	.	
	.	
9	9	9

These two approaches are clearly very different yet the results are the same. The relative merits of algorithms from a machine efficiency point of view have in general been avoided in this text but it is worth mentioning that there can be a substantial difference in machine efficiency terms between the above two strategies. In particular, the synthesis technique lends itself to considerable improvements in execution speed by two simple modifications:

1. In the central test, 'd1*d1*d1' is evaluated for each number whereas the value of 'd1' (the hundreds digit) changes only once in 100 numbers. Similarly, 'd2' remains constant for 10 numbers at a time. In both these cases it is faster to work out the cube of 'd1' and 'd2' in the outer and middle of the three loops respectively, and to use single variables, for example, 'd1cubed' and 'd2cubed', in the test.
2. The value of 'number' is worked out from 'd1', 'd2' and 'd3' each time whereas its value is simply increasing by one. An integer variable, initialised to zero at the outset can be incremented by one each time through the loop.

Implementing a 'super' version of the cubes program is left as an exercise for the reader.

10.5   Using procedures

The most unfortunate consequence of using short examples in introductory programming texts is the lack of encouragement this gives in the use of procedures. Experienced programmers, especially those who are employed to write programs, seldom do write short complete programs and they quickly appreciate the importance of procedures in segmenting the design and coding of a program into manageable proportions. Although still a quite short program in terms of the above, this next example is intended to illustrate how a top-down design process should encourage the programmer to use procedures.

Example 10.5

Write a program to find the average length of words in a sentence.
This is a simple program, typical of much text processing in that the sentence is examined character by character in start to finish order, taking actions based on the values of these characters. We shall assume for simplicity that the words are separated by spaces or the end of lines and that the sentence finishes with a full stop.
An initial design of the algorithm is

begin
      count the total number of letters and words
      calculate and print the average length
end

The average length is simply the number of letters divided by the number of words, but we need to expand the task of counting words and letters:

```
initialise counters 'noofletters' and 'noofwords' to zero
repeat
  read nextchar
  update count of letters and words
until nextchar = full stop
```

Of the two statements in this loop, one of them – 'read nextchar' – maps directly onto a Pascal statement because of the existence of the standard procedure 'read'. In fact, if only we had a procedure called, say, 'updatecount' then the whole of the above design would convert into a Pascal program very easily. Though it may seem unnecessary to take the trouble to define a special procedure in a small exercise like this, in a larger program such decisions are often the key to successful segmentation of complex programming tasks. An important point is that the action of updating the count is a relatively independent task to which the mind can be turned as to a separate programming problem:

```
procedure updatecount;

begin
  if (nextchar = space) or (nextchar = fullstop)
    then noofwords:= noofwords+1
    else noofletters:= noofletters+1
end
```

Note that there is no need to check separately for the end of a line using 'eoln' since Pascal inserts a space as an end of line character. With this procedure declaration, the creation of a complete Pascal program is now only a matter of tidying up the syntax:

```
program averagewordlength (input,output);

const fullstop = '.'; space = ' ';

var nextchar:char;
    noofwords, noofletters:integer;

procedure updatecount;

begin
  if (nextchar = space) or (nextchar = fullstop)
    then noofwords:= noofwords+1
    else noofletters:= noofletters+1
end;

begin
  noofwords:= 0; noofletters:= 0;
```

```
   repeat
      read(nextchar);
      updatecount
   until nextchar = fullstop;
   write('Average wordlength = ',(noofletters/noofwords):8:3)
end.
```

The procedure 'updatecount' operates entirely on global variables in this version and, especially in a larger program where its effect may not be as easy to see, there may be good cases for rewriting the procedure to take in the counts and character to be examined as parameters. From a design viewpoint we use procedures

1. to divide the programming task into self-contained, manageable units which reflect the hierarchical design;
2. to improve program readability;
3. to limit the scope of errors.

In dividing the programming task into relatively small components we are also providing a means of distributing the writing of large programs between two or more programmers. Many large programs perform almost all calculation and input/output within procedures with the consequence that the main program is only a few statements long, calling procedures which in turn call more procedures. Keeping the main program short in this manner makes it considerably easier to understand.

Limiting the scope of errors is vitally important in a larger program. If it is possible to isolate an error to within a specific procedure then the task of correcting it becomes much easier. Indeed, it is not unknown in commercial establishments for 'rogue' procedures to be thrown out and completely rewritten in cases where difficult or recurring errors are discovered.

10.6   Sets and in

It is often useful to be able to check that the value of a variable is one of a particular set of values. To test against a single value is easy by means of the usual relational operators in an **if** statement, as in

if x = 'A'
   then ...

but the condition becomes quite long if there are more than one or two values to test. Consider, for example, the problem of reading a character and printing out whether or not it is a vowel. With a character variable 'ch' the required **if** statement is

> **if** (ch = 'A') **or** (ch = 'E') **or** (ch = 'I') **or**
> (ch = 'O') **or** (ch = 'U')
>   **then** writeln('This is a vowel')
>   **else** writeln('This is not a vowel')

and if we wish to include a test for lower case vowels as well the condition is even longer.

Pascal allows us to specify a set of values of the above type using the construction

> ['A', 'E', 'I', 'O', 'U']

This is called a *constant set*. It becomes particularly useful to us in problems of the kind illustrated by the vowel example when we introduce the special operator 'in', the set inclusion operator. Using **in** we may rephrase the above example as

> **if** ch **in** ['A', 'E', 'I', 'O', 'U']
>   **then** writeln('This is a vowel')
>   **else** writeln('This is not a vowel')

where the expression involving **in** will deliver the value 'true' if the value currently held in 'ch' is a member of the stated set and 'false' otherwise. The resulting expression is not only shorter but reflects more clearly what the programmer is actually trying to do. It is also, as a matter of interest, faster for the computer to execute than the corresponding **if** statement.

The rules state that all members of a set must be constant values of the same type and, reasonably, that the value being tested is also of this type.

Furthermore, the elements must be of a type that Pascal defines as 'ordinal', a classification which includes all the basic types covered in this book except type real. In addition, we can make abbreviations where the constants are successive elements of a type by using two dots, so that the expression

> number **in** [1,2,3,4]

where number is an integer variable may be abbreviated to

> number **in** [1 . .4]

A set may contain a number of such abbreviations as in the following conditional statement which tests to see if 'ch' is an upper or lower case alphabetic character or a digit (assuming usual character set ordering as explained in 6.2):

if ch **in** ['A'..'Z', 'a'..'z', '0'..'9']
    then writeln('This is a letter or a digit')

Note how much clearer this is than the corresponding condition without the set:

if   ((ch > = 'A') **and** (ch < = 'Z')) **or**
    ((ch > = 'a') **and** (ch < = 'z')) **or**
    ((ch > = '0') **and** (ch < = '9'))
      then writeln('This is a letter or a digit')

Example 10.6

Read a sentence terminated by a full stop and print out the number of vowels and consonants.

The algorithm we shall adopt to solve this problem is relatively simple. We do not need to store the entire sentence: it is sufficient to read it character by character, accumulating the sum of the number of vowels and consonants as we go. A first attempt at describing the algorithm is

Initialise vowel and consonant counts to zero

repeat
    read next character
    if character is a vowel
        then add 1 to vowel count
        else if character is a consonant
            then add 1 to consonant count
until character is a full stop

print vowel and consonant counts

Working out if the character is a vowel can be achieved in the manner described earlier but what about identifying a consonant? In fact, this is easy, since if the character is not a vowel we need only test if it is alphabetic to be sure of identifying a consonant. Spaces, punctuation and other non-alphabetic characters are ignored entirely within the loop. There is sufficient detail here to be able to move onto a complete program directly (figure 10.1).

Figure 10.1. The vowels and consonants program.

```pascal
program cvcount (input,output);

var  ch:char;
     vowels, consonants:integer;
begin
  vowels: = 0; consonants: = 0;
  repeat
    read (ch);
    if ch in ['A', 'E', 'I', 'O', 'U', 'a', 'e', 'i', 'o', 'u']
      then vowels: = vowels + 1
      else if ch in ['A'. .'Z', 'a'. .'z']
             then consonants: = consonants + 1
  until ch = '.';
  write('sentence contains', vowels:3, ' vowels and',
  consonants:3, ' consonants')
end.
```

A final word of caution about sets: a given implementation of Pascal will define a maximum number of values in a set and this may be quite small. Usually, the limit will be high enough to allow any sets containing characters but it is unlikely that a set of integers such as [1 . . 1000] will be acceptable.

Exercises

10.1 Write a program based on procedure 'convertgrades' in exercise 7.3 that will read in and average a set of ten letter grades, printing the average itself as a letter grade.

10.2 Write a program to read in the value of a sum of money up to £99.99 and output the value in words as required on a bank cheque. For example, £67.32 will be output as 'sixty seven pounds and 32p only'.

10.3 Write a program to calculate monthly mortgage repayments based on the formula

$$P = \frac{Ar[1+(r/1200)]^{12n}}{1200\{[1+(r/1200)]^{12n}-1\}}$$

where P is the repayment value, A is the amount borrowed, n is the number of years of the loan and r is the annual mortgage interest rate. Include suitable prompts to read in 'A', 'n' and 'r' and print the result to the nearest penny.

As a refinement of this problem, produce a table of repayments for different capital sums and repayment periods. (Hint: you will need to use a **for** statement to calculate the power of 12n.)

10.4 The Soundex Code, developed by Remington Rand, provides a way of reducing similar sounding surnames to a common code. Words are first abbreviated by the following simple rules:

(*a*) Leave the first letter of the name as it is;
(*b*) Omit all subsequent vowels, 'W', 'H' and 'Y';
(*c*) Replace double letters by single (for example, 'TT' becomes 'T');
(*d*) Stop after four characters are produced.

Write a program to read a surname and print out the abbreviated form. For example,

HAWKSLEY   HKSL
LLEWELLYN   LLN

Using more data

All the problems encountered so far have required relatively few items of data – a few simple variables or constants. The emphasis has been on choosing and using the most useful Pascal construction to fit a particular algorithm. In the chapter that follows, the horizon is expanded to include classes of problems that require a larger volume of data to be stored within a program. In particular we look at the technique of storing lists and tables of data in structures called arrays, and at examples of their use.

11.1 Arrays

In section 6.3 we developed a program to read integers and calculate the average. An important characteristic of this program is that we do not need to store the values of all the integers at once. It is sufficient to count the total number of integers and to accumulate their sum in a variable, calculating the average by dividing one by the other. In general, however, it is not difficult to imagine cases in which the above approach is not sufficient. Suppose, for example, we wish to read the same integers and print them in reverse order, or in ascending order perhaps. If we assume that the numbers may only be read once, in the order presented to the input device, then it is clearly necessary to store all numbers inside the computer in the course of obeying the program.

The above assumption about the number of times we may read data and the order in which they appear is a reasonable one in practice. Although most computer systems provide a mechanism for storing input and output data in files (see chapter 12) so that, technically, we may be able to read the same data several times, there are good reasons why we should not normally attempt to do so unless the volume of data was very large.

Neither is it feasible to declare a different integer variable to hold each of the items of data, as suggested by the code below:

.

.

.

var number1, number2, number3, . . . : integer;

.

.

.

read(number1, number2, number3, . . .)

.

.

.

There are two distinct problems here. Firstly, we do not know, in general, how many numbers there will be and, hence, how many variables to declare and read. Secondly, each identifier would have to be processed separately even though the processing may be identical in each case, and this would make programming very long and tedious. Fortunately, this class of problem lends itself neatly to the use of a Pascal facility called the *array*.

An array is a group of items of data of the same type referred to by a single name. An array is ordered, so that we may refer to an individual item in the array by its position – a process called subscripting.

An example will help to explain this process. In common with other data structures, an array identifier is introduced in a **var** declaration such as

var numbers: **array** [1 . . 10] **of** integer;

Pictorially, this introduces a data structure of the form shown in figure 11.1.

Each of the elements of this array may hold an integer and a particular element is identified by its subscript, thus

Figure 11.1. **array** 'numbers'.

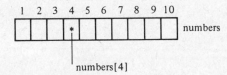

numbers[4]

numbers[1]   refers to the first integer
numbers[4]   refers to the fourth integer
numbers[i]   refers to the ith integer

Note the use of square brackets in array declarations and in subscripting.

The last example is particularly interesting in that the subscript is a variable ('i'). Here, 'i' must be an integer variable with a value within the range of subscripts for the array; between 1 and 10 inclusive in this case. By assigning a value to 'i' during program execution we have a powerful means of accessing whichever element of the array we choose. Moreover, the subscript may be any expression that evaluates to a value in the correct subscript range. Thus, in addition to the above three,

numbers[i + 1]
numbers[2*i + 3]

are also examples of *subscripted variables*.

In a program statement we may use an element of an array in basically the same way as a simple variable. A subscripted variable can appear on the left of an assignment statement, for example, as in

numbers[1]: = 25

or

numbers[i]: = 2

in which the values shown are stored in elements of the array. Similarly, in expressions, we may write subscripted variables in places where simple ones could appear, as in

numbers[i] + numbers[i + 1]

or

3*(numbers[6 − i] + 10)

Arrays may be formed of elements of any type but the number of elements in the array must be constant. The length of the array and the range of subscripts is defined within square brackets in the array declaration by means of an *index type*. Thus, in the declaration of 'numbers', the index type is

1 . . 10

(a subrange of integer type) meaning that only values that fall within this subset of integers may form legitimate subscripts.

Consistent with our practice of making programs as well-constructed and readable as possible, it is better to eliminate '10' in favour of a constant identifier and, depending on the likelihood of a future change, to do the same for the '1':

const lownum = 1; highnum = 10;

and to declare the array as:

var numbers: **array** [lownum . . highnum] **of** integer;

There are, in fact, a variety of possible ways of declaring the same array in Pascal and an alternative is described later in this chapter.

Use of **const** identifiers in the array declaration has the advantage that sensibly named identifiers are available for later use to represent the smallest and largest permissible subscripts (called the *lower* and *upper array bounds*). In practice, as long as all references to the upper bound use 'highnum' and not '10', for example, it is a simple matter to modify the program later to cater for an array of, say, 20 numbers by changing only the **const** value.

As a further example of an array declaration, the following introduces an array of 120 characters:

const maxletters = 120;
var sentence: **array** [1 . . maxletters] **of** char;

11.2   Using arrays

Given the ability to declare arrays in the above manner, let us look at an example of how they can be used and, in particular, how an element of an array is identified by means of a subscript (also referred to as an index).

Example 11.1
Write a program to recognise palindromes.

A palindrome is a word or phrase that reads the same forwards and backwards and we shall stick rigidly to this definition, such that 'ABBA' and 'ABLE WAS I ERE I SAW ELBA' are acceptable palindromes, but 'MADAM I'M ADAM' is not. We shall test for a perfect reversal in the second half of the phrase, including spaces and punctuation. Further, it is assumed that the user will type in the phrase to be tested.

An array is proposed in this example because we cannot start to test for a palindrome until the entire phrase has been read by the program. We need to find the middle of the phrase and this is impossible until all of it has been read. Here is the outline of an algorithm:

Read the phrase.

Compare pairs of letters from the start and end of the phrase, working in towards the middle.

If the middle is reached and all pairs of letters are identical, the phrase is a palindrome.

The rather ambiguous middle statement in this description is illustrated more clearly in figure 11.2. Using an array of characters to hold each letter of the phrase in a separate element of the array, the pairs of letters to be compared are marked. Of course this particular example fails to satisfy the condition in the last part of our algorithm and will be rejected as a palindrome.

A suitable array for the phrase is required. The type of each element is clearly the Pascal standard data type 'char' but the number of elements needed is less obvious. We must choose an array length that is sufficiently large to accommodate the largest phrase to be tested and use our judgement in picking this value. Since a typical maximum length of input line from a computer terminal is 80 characters, let us choose this as the limit and assume in addition that a phrase will be terminated by the end of a line. In accepting this limit the author is aware that palindromes of several hundred characters in length have been written!

We may declare the array:

> **const** maxindex = 80;
> **var** phrase : **array** [1 . . maxindex] **of** char;

To return now to the algorithm, we first read the entire phrase into the array. Some kind of loop is needed for this since we must read the characters one by one and place them in successive elements of 'phrase'.

A suitable read loop is

> i := 0;
> **while not** eoln **do**
> **begin**
>   i := i + 1;
>   read(phrase[i])
> **end**;

Figure 11.2. Comparing letter pairs.

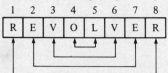

The integer variable 'i' is used as a subscript identifying the elements 'phrase[1]', 'phrase[2]' and so on, into which characters are placed. The standard Boolean Pascal variable 'eoln' will remain false until the end of the line is reached after reading the last character in the phrase.

The actual task of checking the phrase can now be performed. Two further variables 'lower' and 'upper' are introduced to hold the subscripts of the elements being compared. They are initialised to the positions of the first and last characters in 'phrase'.

```
lower:= 1; upper:= i;
while (lower < upper) and (phrase[lower] = phrase[upper]) do
   begin
      lower:= lower + 1;
      upper:= upper − 1
   end;
```

Note that pairs of letters are tested for equality, working towards the middle. The loop stops when either the middle is reached ('lower' is no longer less than 'upper') or two letters are compared and found to be different. On exit from the loop we can tell easily whether the phrase is a palindrome. If it is, then the middle of the phrase will have been reached and 'lower' will be greater than, or equal to, 'upper'. This is used to print an appropriate message:

```
if lower > = upper
   then write('is a palindrome')
   else write('is not a palindrome')
```

The complete program is given below:

```
program palindrome (input, output);
const maxindex = 80;
var  i, upper, lower:integer;
     phrase:array [1 . . maxindex] of char;
begin
   i:= 0;
   while not eoln do
      begin
         i:= i + 1;
         read(phrase[i])
      end;
   lower:= 1; upper:= i;
```

```
    while (lower < upper) and (phrase[lower] = phrase[upper]) do
    begin
        lower:= lower+1;
        upper:= upper-1
    end;
    if lower > = upper
        then write('is a palindrome')
        else write('is not a palindrome')

end.
```

Having worked through the palindrome example this is a reasonable point to question what would happen if a line of more than 80 ('maxindex') characters were presented at the input to the above program. The **while** loop reading each character in turn would reach a point where an assignment to 'phrase[81]' is attempted; an element which does not exist. This is usually referred to as an 'array bound error' or as 'array bound overflow' and the condition may be detected as an error resulting in program termination.

Unfortunately, an array bound error may also occur in the above program if an empty line is provided (that is, if 'return' is the first key typed). The reason is that 'eoln' is true immediately and the **while** loop is never executed at all. Thus, 'i' is zero, this is assigned to 'upper', and an attempt is made to access 'phrase[upper]' which is again outside the bounds of 'phrase'.

As an aside, note that run-time checking for errors such as this and also for arithmetic overflow, for example, costs time, and most compilers make such checking optional. Always ensure that all possible checking is included during program development and then, perhaps, leave checks out if you wish to increase the speed of a well tested program. The method of turning checks on and off must be ascertained from local documentation.

More specifically, we could improve the reliability of the above program by changing the **while** condition to

```
    while not eoln and (i < > maxindex)
```

and even include a test to print out an error message of our own if more than 80 characters are entered. If required, an **if** statement could be included to pick up the empty line case, as suggested by

```
    if upper < > 0
        then begin
            while (lower < upper) and (phrase[lower] = phrase[upper]) do
            . . .
```

11.3 Sorting

One of the commonest computational processes of all is sorting: re-ordering a set of data values in a particular way. As mentioned earlier, in order to sort a list of numbers it is not sufficient to read and process the numbers one by one. We consider here the use of an array to hold an entire list during the sort.

Sorting is so important in computing that a number of complete books have been written on the subject. There is no one ideal sorting algorithm for every case: some methods work better than others if the data are known to be partially sorted already, for example, while others may be inadvisable for large volumes of data. Thus, the technique shown below is not universally suitable; it is a relatively simple algorithm, however.

Example 11.2

Read a list of 20 real numbers and print them in descending order. It is easy to divide this task into three stages:

Read 20 numbers into an array.
Sort the array.
Print the array.

A suitable array to hold the numbers may be declared in similar fashion to the 'numbers' array defined earlier, though this time the elements are of type real:

```
const hiindex = 20;
var nums:array [1 . . hiindex] of real;
```

As the numbers are presented to the input device we would like them to be read and placed in successive elements of the array 'nums': 'nums[1]', 'nums[2]' and so on.

We can use a **for** loop with an integer control variable 'i' to do this reading:

```
for i: = 1 to hiindex do
    read(nums[i])
```

The **for** statement is very useful in stepping through successive elements of an array in this manner. Indeed, an almost identical loop can be used to write out the sorted numbers later:

```
for i: = 1 to hiindex do
    write(nums[i])
```

One method of sorting an array is called the straight exchange technique.

Values in the array are re-ordered by an algorithm which exchanges pairs of values in a series of passes (sweeps) through the array. The first sweep achieves the following:

> Scan the array to find the position of the largest number.
> Exchange the values in this and the first position of the array.

Thus, at the end of this sweep, the largest number is moved to 'nums[1]'. A second sweep is now performed, starting at the second element in the array, in order to locate the largest remaining number and to exchange it with 'nums[2]'. It is evident that if we continue with further sweeps, the array will be sorted after the nineteenth sweep (the smallest two numbers will be correctly sorted after this sweep). To illustrate what is happening, figure 11.3 shows positions of numbers in an array after successive sweeps (an array of length 5 is used for brevity). Note that if the remaining largest number is already at the start position of a sweep, as in figure 11.3 sweep 4, an element is exchanged with itself. In practice, we may assume that this occurs too infrequently to warrant special attention, and we shall treat this case in exactly the same way as any other exchange. The structure of the sort algorithm may now be defined, using a **for** statement to control the sweeping:

Figure 11.3. Exchange sorting.

11.6	2.1	15.9	3.25	6.6	Initial data

15.9	2.1	11.6	3.25	6.6	After sweep 1

15.9	11.6	2.1	3.25	6.6	After sweep 2

15.9	11.6	6.6	3.25	2.1	After sweep 3

15.9	11.6	6.6	3.25	2.1	After sweep 4

```
for sweep: = 1 to hiindex − 1 do
  begin
    find largest number from nums[sweep] to end of array
    exchange this with the number in nums[sweep]
  end
```

Finding the largest number is again a candidate for a **for** loop. Using the variables 'bignum' and 'bigindex' to hold values and their position (index) in the array, the above design may be turned into Pascal as

```
for sweep: = 1 to hiindex − 1 do
  begin
    {find largest}
    bignum: = nums[sweep]; bigindex: = sweep;
    for i: = sweep + 1 to hiindex do
        if nums[i] > bignum
          then begin
                   bignum: = nums[i]; bigindex: = i
               end;
    {exchange}
    nums[bigindex]: = nums[sweep];
    nums[sweep]: = bignum
  end
```

Consider also why the order of the two statements in the exchange sequence is important: we must not overwrite the contents of one element before it has been copied to its new position in the array.

Note how this algorithm picks the first element in a sweep as the current largest and then updates the choice if a larger one is found in the scan loop. The complete program is given in figure 11.4.

Figure 11.4. The sort program.
```
program sort (input,output);

const hiindex = 20;

var  sweep, bigindex, i: integer;
     bignum: real;
     nums: array [1 . . hiindex] of real;

begin
  for i: = 1 to hiindex do
      read(nums[i]);
  for sweep: = 1 to hiindex − 1 do
```

```
begin
  {find largest}
  bignum: = nums[sweep]; bigindex: = sweep;
  for i: = sweep + 1 to hiindex do
    if nums[i] > bignum
      then begin
             bignum: = nums[i]; bigindex: = i
           end;
  {exchange}
  nums[bigindex]: = nums[sweep];
  nums[sweep]: = bignum
end;
for i: = 1 to hiindex do
  write(nums[i]: 8: 2)
end.
```

The sort program may be modified easily to accept a greater or fewer number of numbers – only 'hiindex' need be changed.

11.4   Tables of data

As mentioned earlier, we can declare arrays of any type of element. Indeed, the elements themselves may be other arrays as shown in the declaration below.

```
const rows = 4; cols = 3;
var table: array [1..rows] of array [1..cols] of char;
```

It is convenient to think of the resulting data structure in terms of rows

Figure 11.5. A two-dimensional array.

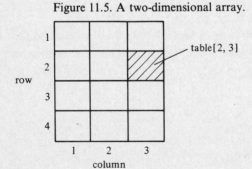

and columns as the diagram in figure 11.5 illustrates. This is a two-dimensional structure containing 12 elements organised in such a way that any element is identified by a pair of subscripts, one each for the row and column of the element. In practice, the rather long-winded declaration of 'table' above is usually abbreviated to

var table:**array** [1 . . rows, 1 . . cols] **of** char;

in which the types specifying the dimensions of the array are separated by a comma inside the square brackets. In any subsequent array subscripting, the row and column subscripts are also written in square brackets in this order and separated by a comma as shown by the shaded element 'table[2,3]' in the diagram.

As with one-dimensional arrays, one or both of the subscripts may be variable and **for** statements are particularly useful to step through elements of a two-dimensional array. For example, two **for** statements can be used to set every element to a particular character value:

```
for i: = 1 to rows do
   for j: = 1 to cols do
      table[i,j]: = 'A'
```

If this seems confusing, consider the order in which the elements will be assigned the value 'A'. Initially, 'i' is set to 1 in the outer loop; 'j' to 1 in the inner and 'A' is assigned to 'table[1,1]'. Next, the control variable of the inner loop, 'j', is increased to 2 and the assignment is repeated for 'table[1,2]'. An assignment to table[1,3] follows, at which point the inner loop is completed and it is the turn of 'i' in the outer loop to be increased to 2. The inner loop is repeated three times more to fill in 'table[2,1]', 'table[2,2]' and 'table[2,3]'. This is continued with subscript values [3,1], [3,2], [3,3], [4,1], [4,2] and finally [4,3].

Example 11.3
Print the words in a letter 'square'.

The letter 'square' in question is in fact a table of letters such as that in figure 11.6 in which words are formed both across and down the table.

We shall assume that the letters for the table will be entered in row order without gaps, thus

MAPAXEILLLET

and endeavour to print out all seven words in the table.

The array 'table' declared earlier is quite suitable to hold all the letters.

Reading the letters in is also very similar to the example in which the letter 'A' was placed in the elements of 'table' except that this time we must read the characters to be entered:

```
for i:= 1 to rows do
    for j:= 1 to cols do
        read(table[i,j])
```

Printing the horizontal words requires a similar nested loop structure, taking care to insert a new line only between the printing of each row so that the words appear on separate lines:

```
for i:= 1 to rows do
    begin
        for j:= 1 to cols do
            write(table[i,j]);
        writeln
    end
```

For the vertical words it is only necessary to reverse the loops so that each column is printed in turn:

```
for j:= 1 to cols do
    begin
        for i:= 1 to rows do
            write(table[i,j]);
        writeln
    end
```

The complete program is given in figure 11.7

Figure 11.6. A letter 'square'.

M	A	P
A	X	E
I	L	L
L	E	T

Figure 11.7. The letter 'square' program.

```
program lettersquare (input,output);
const rows = 4; cols = 3;
var  i,j:integer;
     table:array [1..rows, 1..cols] of char;
```

```
begin
  for i: = 1 to rows do
    for j: = 1 to cols do
        read(table[i,j]);
  writeln;
  {print rows}
  for i: = 1 to rows do
    begin
      for j: = 1 to cols do
          write(table[i,j]);
      writeln
    end;

  {print cols}
  for j: = 1 to cols do
    begin
      for i: = 1 to rows do
          write(table[i,j]);
      writeln
    end
end.
```

Example 11.4
Print a magic square.

We wish to produce a square of numbers this time with the 'magical' property that all rows, columns and diagonals add up to the same number. A 3×3 example is shown in figure 11.8.

Figure 11.8. A magic square.

6	1	8
7	5	3
2	9	4

row, column and diagonal
sum = 15

This, and even larger squares, look impressive and with each number from 1 upwards used once and once only, they would seem to be particularly difficult to produce. In fact, providing we limit ourselves to squares with an odd number of rows and columns there is a fairly simple algorithm to generate a square. In informal terms it goes as follows:

1. Place a 1 in the middle of the top row.

2. Move, or attempt to move, one position diagonally up left and
   (a) If the movement was from the top left-hand corner square then place the next number underneath the corner position else
   (b) If the new position is above the top row then place the next number at the bottom of the new column else
   (c) If the new position is to the left of the left-hand column then place the next number at the right-hand end of the new row else
   (d) If the new position is already occupied then place the new number beneath the previous number else
   (e) Place the next number in the new position.

3. If the square is not full, repeat from step 2.

The algorithm, written as it is in English, is open to misinterpretation and it is wise to check it against the 3×3 square above to make sure it is fully understood. It is a good example of why English is not a good language with which to program a computer!

Consider a program to calculate and print a 5×5 square. The square itself is clearly a case for representation by a two-dimensional Pascal array which we can declare as

```
const oddsize = 5;
var square: array [1 . . oddsize, 1 . . oddsize] of integer;
```

Since the algorithm involves moving from place to place in the square we shall introduce a pair of integer variables, 'row' and 'col' to use as subscripts marking the present position in the array. These are initialised to the centre of the top row in the first step of the algorithm by

```
row: = 1;
col: = oddsize div 2 + 1;
square[row,col]: = 1
```

remembering that **div** produces the integer result of division with the remainder ignored.

Steps 2 and 3 of the algorithm combine to form a loop in which a new number is placed in the square each time through. The numbers range from 2 up to the number that is equal to the number of positions in the square ($=$ oddsize^2) and a **for** statement is a particularly suitable means of expressing this sequence of numbers.

A problem arises in determining whether a position is occupied or not in step 2 of the algorithm. When an array is declared, space is allocated for the elements in the computer store but no initial values are given to the elements: they may contain rubbish left over from the previous program, for example. Thus, the only way we can safely test if a position is occupied by a number placed there by our program is to initialise all the elements in the square to a special 'unoccupied' value before we start placing the numbers. We can use zero, for example, to denote an unoccupied position since zero is not one of the numbers to be placed. We can define the entire algorithm as

> Clear all elements of 'square' to zero
>
> Place a 1 in the middle of the top row
>
> **for** nextnumber$:=$ 2 **to** sqr(oddsize) **do**
>   place the next number
>
> Print the square.

To place a number we first make the attempted move diagonally up left by manipulating the subscripts:

> row$:=$ row-1;   col$:=$ col-1

The rest of the positioning is then conditional on the new value of these subscripts:

```
if (row < 1) and (col < 1)   {rule 2a}
   then begin
        row:= 2;   col:= 1
   end
else if row < 1   {rule 2b}
     then row:= oddsize
     else if col < 1   {rule 2c}
          then col:= oddsize
          else if square[row,col] < > 0   {rule 2d}
               then begin
                    row:= row+2; col:= col+1
               end;
```

Note that this conditional statement is only responsible for repositioning the subscript to the position of the next number and thus rule 2e is achieved by default since no repositioning is required. Having calculated the new position the new number is placed in the array:

square[row,col]: = nextnumber

'Clearing' the array and printing it out are further examples of nested **for** statements, as can be seen in the complete program in figure 11.9.

```
program magic (input,output);

const oddsize = 5;

var row, col, nextnumber : integer;
    square : array [1..oddsize, 1..oddsize] of integer;

begin
 {clear array}
 for row := 1 to oddsize do
  for col := 1 to oddsize do square[row,col] := 0;
 {place 1}
 row := 1; col := oddsize div 2+1; square[row,col] := 1;

 for nextnumber := 2 to sqr(oddsize) do
  begin
   row := row - 1; col := col - 1;
   if (row < 1) and (col < 1) {top left corner case}
    then begin
         row := 2; col := 1
         end
    else if row < 1 {off top row}
         then row := oddsize
         else if col < 1 {off left column}
              then col := oddsize
              else if square[row,col] <> 0
                        {occupied square}
                   then begin
                        row := row+2; col := col+1
                        end;
    {place next number}
    square[row,col] := nextnumber
   end;

   {print square}
   for row := 1 to oddsize do
       begin
       for col := 1 to oddsize do
           write (square[row,col]:4);
       writeln
       end

end.
```

Figure 11.9. The magic square program.

11.5   Array **and** type
When 'x' is defined in the declaration:

var x:**array** [1 . . 6] **of** integer;

it becomes a variable of a new data type (**array** [1 . . 6] **of** integer). Arrays are the first examples we have encountered of where the programmer can extend the range of types provided as standard (integer, real, etc.) by defining new ones. They are by no means the only new types possible and we shall meet some more shortly. Firstly, however, let us note that it is possible to name a type using a new kind of declaration headed by the reserved word '**type**':

type sixarry = **array** [1 . . 6] **of** integer;

The effect is to provide a type identifier 'sixarry' which is syntactically equivalent to 'integer', 'real', etc. in that it can be used later to declare variables of the new type, as in

var x:sixarry;

The ordering of declarations is such that **type** comes immediately before **var** declarations but after any **const** declarations.

Why should we ever bother to use **type** when a perfectly acceptable direct way of declaring a variable such as 'x' above is open to us? In essence, the answer is once again largely because it improves the structure of a program. Since new types form an integral part of the data structuring of a program it is better to declare them once and for all near the top of the program. A more down to earth reason is that 'user-defined' types *must* be declared in this manner if it is intended that procedures or functions that have parameters of these types be written. The following procedure, for example, could be written to print the values in any array of type 'sixarry':

```
procedure printsix (var sixno:sixarry);
var i:integer;
begin
    for i:= 1 to 6 do write(sixno[i])
end;
```

and it is not permissible to write '**array** [1 . . 6] **of** integer' in place of 'sixarry'. Note that a **var** parameter is used for the array. This may seem odd at first sight since 'sixno' is clearly an input parameter to the procedure and no element of the array is altered. If the '**var**' is omitted, however, the rules for passing the resulting value parameter would force a copy of the actual parameter to be made on calling the procedure and copying an array can involve substantial overheads, particularly if it is large. This is one case where the use of a particular mechanism can make a sizeable difference to program efficiency without otherwise affecting the choice of algorithm. The exception to the parameter rules in section 7.3 to cover arrays should read

> Make all array parameters 'var' unless you actually do require a physical copy to be made.

A copy will only be necessary if you intend to make alterations to elements of the array within the procedure that must not affect the original array.

The general syntax of **type** (see appendix 1) is similar in many ways to that of **const**. Extending the principle of defining types further, it is also possible to declare a new type to be a subrange of an existing type, as in

> **type** sixint = 1..6;

'sixint' is called a *subrange type* and from the nature of the declaration it is known to be a subrange of integer. Subranges of characters are also possible; for example,

> **type** letter = 'A'..'Z';
> digit = '0'..'9';

but a subrange of real is not permitted.

Given such definitions we may use the new types in declarations, as in the example below:

> **var** sixarry2:**array** [sixint] **of** integer;
> i:sixint;

In this last example, 'i' would be a particularly good variable to use as an index to 'sixarry2'. Only values between 1 and 6 inclusive may be assigned to 'i', making it impossible to index the array with a subscript whose value is outside the bounds of the array. Any errors in assigning to 'i' will cause the program to terminate with a recognisable error message at that point rather than to go on to attempt to access a non-existent array element.

A second example illustrates that the index type of an array may be other than a subrange of integer:

> **var** alpharray:**array** [letter] **of** integer;

where 'letter' is a subrange of 'char' as defined above. The resulting array contains 26 integer locations (assuming 'A'–'Z' are consecutive in the character set) and may be indexed by, for example, a char variable containing an upper-case letter, as in

```
ch = 'B';            {'ch' of type char}
alpharray[ch]: = 0;  {the second element of the array}
```

If required, all elements of 'alpharray' could be set to zero using:

for ch: = 'A' **to** 'Z' **do** alpharray[ch]: = 0

Finally, note the following alternative declarations for the earlier 'lettersquare' program making use of **type** declarations:

```
program lettersquare (input,output);
const rows = 4; cols = 3;
type  rowtype = 1 . . rows;
      coltype = 1 . . cols;
var i: rowtype; j: coltype;
    table: array [rowtype,coltype] of char;
```

Exercises

11.1 Modify the sort program in figure 11.4 so that it sorts 20 *characters* into *ascending* alphabetical order.

11.2 Write a program to read a sentence and print each word backwards.

11.3 In a game of bridge there are four players. Each player is dealt 13 cards and may make a number of bids to form a contract with his playing partner. As an aid to assessing the strength of a hand a player may count the number of 'points' in the hand according to the following scale:

Ace – 4 points; King – 3 points; Queen – 2 points; Jack – 1 point; Void (no cards in a suit) – 2 points; Singleton (1 card only in a suit) – 1 point.

Write a program which includes separate procedures to perform the following tasks:

1. Read a hand.
2. Calculate points in a hand.
3. Print a hand.

The output should be in conventional form as illustrated in

S   A K J 10 7 3
H   2
D   –
C   K Q 9 8 4 3

16 Points

You may assume that the hand has been sorted into suits such that the data for the above hand would be

S A K J 10 7 3 H 2 D – C K Q 9 8 4 3

11.4 Extend the Soundex Code (exercise (10.4)) to produce a four character representation of a name from the abbreviated form as follows:

1. Leave the first character as it is.

2. Replace the next three characters of the abbreviated name by digits, according to the table

B,F,P,V	1
C,G,J,K,Q,S,X,Z	2
D,T	3
L	4
M,N	5
R	6

3. For short names, fill out with zeros.

Test the effectiveness of the code by reading and comparing pairs of names that sound the same but are spelled differently. For example,

BENNETT, BENNET, BENETT, BENNITT = B530
STEVENS, STEPHENS, STIEVENS = S315

11.5 The simplest kind of encoding algorithm exchanges the letters in a message by others on a one-for-one basis; for example, 'E' is replaced by 'T', etc. Write a program that will read the 26 replacement characters for 'A' to 'Z' and encode a short upper-case only message.

Write a decoding program for the encoded messages.

Text processing and files

I have made this letter longer than usual, only because I have not had the time to make it shorter.
Lettres Provinciales, Blaise Pascal

The term *text processing* embraces a very wide group of problems linked by the common theme that they are concerned with the (usually large scale) manipulation of non-numerical data. In one sense, text processing suggests the analysis of tracts of natural language from a linguistic point of view – the example in the last chapter of vowel and consonant counting is a simple one – and, indeed, the computer has proved to be a powerful tool in this work. In practice, an astonishing number of other computer applications are concerned almost uniquely with processing text in one form or another. This is the case in *word processing*, for example, where the computer is used to assist in the preparation of correspondence and other documents, and also in the rapidly expanding field of information retrieval.

From a programming viewpoint, most of these applications have a great deal in common as the selection of examples presented in this chapter will show. First of all, the concept of a file is introduced since this is central to all processing of large volumes of data whether they be text-based or numeric.

12.1   Files

Earlier programs in this book which required external data used the read statement as a means of requesting the user to enter appropriate values. This approach is unsuitable if the volume of data is very large and may be tedious with even quite small data sets if frequent re-running of the program on the same, or similar, data is to be carried out. In most

137

of the above cases it is desirable to store the required data in a relatively permanent way in a *file* on the computer and to be able to read data from or write data to this file. Files established in this way are stored on a *backing store*, such as a magnetic disc or tape, where the data can be retained securely for long periods or even removed completely from the computer system for safe keeping or transfer to another computer.

To be consistent, we refer to any coherent stream of data associated with a Pascal program as a file, whether or not it is kept on backing store. Thus, for example, the data output from a program and printed on a VDU is a file, though it appears on a screen, not magnetic disc, and is not saved for future use. Similarly, characters typed on a VDU keyboard to satisfy requests for data from read statements in a program form an input file.

We have already used two files implicitly in earlier examples in association with 'read' and 'write'. They are called 'input' and 'output', respectively. These two standard input and output streams in Pascal are special in the sense that 'read' and 'write' are connected to them without further action on the part of the programmer.

Though files in Pascal may contain data of many types, by far the most common is the *text file* which as its name suggests consists entirely of characters. Any file produced by typing from a keyboard, for example, will be a text file as will output data that are to be presented on a character-based peripheral such as a VDU or printer. Text files account for the vast majority of data files used on a computer and we shall concentrate exclusively on these.

Unseen by the Pascal programmer who specifies *input* or *output* in the program heading is an implicit declaration made effectively at the beginning of every program:

   var input,output:text;

where 'text' is another standard type, like 'integer' or 'real', but in this case, an item of type 'text' is a 'file of char' rather than a simple integer or real number. Not only are the text files 'input' and 'output' declared implicitly in this way but calls of, for example,

   read(x)

or

   write(x)

are assumed to refer to reading 'x' from input and writing 'x' to output respectively. A text file should be visualised as a continuous stream of characters together with a pointer marking the current position in the stream; for example, 'input' text file

start   finish

the cat sat on the mat.

current
pointer

At this point, the statement 'read(x)', if 'x' is declared as a char variable, has the effect of reading the next character ('a') into 'x' and also of moving the pointer over the item just read so that it now points to the 't' in 'cat'. In a similar fashion, writing a character to output effectively tags that character onto the end of the stream of characters destined for the output text file.

For reading and writing characters to and from data files of type 'text' the process is straightforward. In fact, we know that 'read' and 'write' can be used with data types other than 'char' and we must extend the above argument to cover this. With numbers, integer or real, a series of automatic conversions are applied by the Pascal system to turn characters from the input into numerical representation for use within the program and to turn internal numbers back into strings of characters for output purposes. Thus, the integer equivalent of the last example is

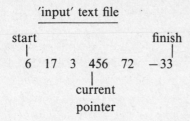

'input' text file

start   finish

6   17   3   456   72   −33

current
pointer

The statement 'read(i)', where 'i' is declared as an integer variable, must invoke a conversion of the characters '4', '5' and '6' into the integer '456' which is then stored in 'i'. Once again the pointer moves over the characters read to be left pointing at the space after '456'.

This linear view of input and output files is modified slightly because we humans often prefer our files to be structured in one way or another. Usually we divide files into lines of data and we may wish to refer to the line structure within a program. It is for this reason that the routines 'readln', 'writeln', and the Boolean function 'eoln' were introduced in chapter 8.

In many applications it is desirable to have more than the two standard files and we can declare new text files in Pascal by introducing variables of type 'text':

>**var** infile, outfile:text;

Before use in a program the state of a file must be initialised with either *reset* (an input file) or *rewrite* (an output file):

>reset(infile);
>rewrite(outfile)

Note once again that 'input' and 'output' are initialised in this way 'behind the scenes'.

To read data from the new input file 'infile' we use the familiar 'read' or 'readln' procedures with an extra parameter:

>read(infile,x)

The first parameter is the name of the text file on which that operation is to be performed. Special treatment is given to 'input': its name is assumed in the absence of another file name such that

>read(x) is an abbreviation of read(input,x)

Similarly, the name of the output file must be written as the first parameter in a 'write' or 'writeln' statement unless its name is 'output', since

>write(x) is an abbreviation of write(output,x)

An example of an output statement to a file other than 'output' is

>writeln(outfile,'Some text',x,x*2)

It was mentioned earlier that input/output in Pascal is handled in the same way regardless of what external physical device (keyboard, printer, disc file, etc.) is providing or receiving the data. How then do we achieve the link between a Pascal file (for example, 'input' or 'output') and an external source or destination? The answer lies partly in Pascal and partly in the operating system commands used to compile and run Pascal programs on your computer.

It is the job of the Pascal language to define and initialise text files for input or output as shown above. In addition, all file names should be written in the program heading, as in

>**program** fourfile (input, infile, output, outfile);

A way in which these Pascal file names may be linked to actual external files on the computer is not yet defined in the ISO standard for Pascal and, hence, the various approaches adopted are extremely machine-dependent.

A 'file' in this sense may be a disk file or a peripheral such as the keyboard, screen or a printer. To set up this external link it is necessary to consult the documentation for your particular computer. Note that it is not necessary to make such an external link if a file is used only temporarily by a program: if data are written to a file which is then reset to allow the data to be read later in the same program. Such temporary files disappear on completion of the program.

12.2 String manipulation

The program below is used to illustrate two programming techniques. Firstly, it is concerned almost entirely with rearranging strings of characters from input to output, with minimal internal processing. Additionally, the input data are assumed to be held in a file and not typed in when the program is executed.

Example 12.1
'Old Macdonald had a farm'

Write a program that will read the animals and noises for the verses in the above song and print out the complete lyrics.

'Old Macdonald had a farm' is a typical example of a song in which each verse ends by repeating lines from all previous verses. If you are unfamiliar with the song it will help to read the sample of expected output from the program in figure 12.3 at this point. In the early stages of program design we look for similarities between verses in order to reduce the number of separate write operations required:

read the animal noises from the file

repeat for all verses: write one verse

We shall assume that a file containing the names of the animals and their noises has been created on the computer to be used in the form shown in figure 12.1.

Figure 12.1. Noises and animals.

chick
quack
gobble   4 noises
moo

chicks
ducks
turkeys   4 animals
cows

The method of creating this data file depends on the operating system you are using. This ordering of the noises and animals is important because they are not used in the same way. The name of each animal is used just once, in the order shown above, but the noises are used many times. To permit this frequent reference to a noise we shall read all noises into an array at the start of the program but read the animal names only when they are required.

Since all the data in this program are to be read from only one source (the above file) it would be possible to reassign 'input' to read from the file without defining a new data file at all. In general, however, it is more usual to require additional input from, say, the keyboard of a terminal: perhaps to read the number of verses to be printed, for example. To allow for the possibility of future modifications of this nature a new text file is declared and initialised:

```
program lyrics (input,output,farmyard);

var farmyard:text;

begin
    reset(farmyard, 'oldmac');  {a typical way of connecting farm-
        .                         yard to a disk file called oldmac in
        .                         order to read from it}
        .
```

To read in the animal noises we need an array in which to hold them – a two-dimensional array of char –

```
var noises:array [1 . . verses,1 . . 8] of char;
```

We shall define the number of verses in the song as a constant at the top of the program. A loop will be required to read in the animal noises and here the problem is that they are not all 8 characters long. The simplest solution is to fill out with spaces:

```
for i:= 1 to verses do
    begin
        j:= 1;
        while not eoln(farmyard) do
            begin read(farmyard, noises[i,j]); j:= j+1 end;
        for k:= j to 8 do noises[i,k]:= ' ';
        readln(farmyard)
    end
```

noting that 'readln(farmyard)' forces a move of the input pointer to the start of the next line to be ready for the next 'noise'.

We are now ready to develop the main printing algorithm:

> **for** verse:= 1 **to** verses **do**
>   write one verse

Writing one verse involves three kinds of character strings:

(a) Unvarying text, for example, 'Old Macdonald had a farm';
(b) Animal names;
(c) Animal noises.

We can easily cater for (a) by writing the text out directly as a string in a write or writeln statement, and (b) simply requires us to read the next animal from the file 'farmyard' and to print this directly. Note that following the reading of the animal noises the input pointer is left pointing to the first character of the first animal. Output of (c), the animal noises, occurs several times in a verse and it will pay us to write a special procedure to print the noise appropriate for a given verse number, together with a following space:

> **procedure** printnoise (noiseno:integer);
>
> **var** col:integer;
>
> **begin**
>   col:= 0;
>   **repeat**
>   col:= col+1;
>   write(noises[noiseno,col])
>   **until** noises[noiseno,col] = ' '
> **end**;

The rest of the program is a matter of working through the necessary use of (a), (b) and (c) types of output above and the entire program is given in figure 12.2.

Figure 12.2. The lyrics program.

```
program lyrics (input,output,farmyard);

const verses = 4 ;

var farmyard : text;
    verse,vline,i,j,k : integer;
    ch : char;
    noises : array [1..verses,1..8] of char;

procedure printnoise (noiseno : integer);
var col : integer;
```

```
begin
 col := 0;
 repeat
  col := col + 1;
  write(noises[noiseno,col])
 until noises[noiseno,col] = ' '
end;

begin
 reset(farmyard,'oldmac');
 {read noises}
 for i := 1 to verses do
  begin
   j := 1;
   while not eoln(farmyard) do
    begin read(farmyard,noises[i,j]); j := j+1 end;
   for k := j to 8 do noises[i,k] := ' ';
   readln(farmyard)
  end;

 {print verses}
 for verse := 1 to verses do
  begin
   writeln('Old Macdonald had a farm, E-I-E-I-O,');
   write('And on this farm he had some ');
   repeat read(farmyard,ch); write(ch) until eoln(farmyard);
   readln(farmyard);
   writeln(', E-I-E-I-O');
   {Now write out this, and previous noises}
   for vline := verse downto 1 do
    begin
     write('With a ');
     printnoise(vline); printnoise(vline);
     write('here, and a ');
     printnoise(vline); printnoise(vline);
     writeln('there,');
     write('Here a '); printnoise(vline);
     write('there a '); printnoise(vline);
     write('everywhere a '); printnoise(vline);
     if vline <> 1 then writeln
    end;
   {add last line to verse}
   printnoise(1); writeln;
   writeln('Old Macdonald had a farm E-I-E-I-O.');
   writeln
  end {of print one verse}
end.
```

Figure 12.3. Sample output from the lyrics program.

```
Old Macdonald had a farm, E-I-E-I-O,
And on this farm he had some chicks, E-I-E-I-O
With a chick chick here, and a chick chick there,
Here a chick there a chick everywhere a chick chick
Old Macdonald had a farm E-I-E-I-O.
```

```
Old Macdonald had a farm, E-I-E-I-O,
And on this farm he had some ducks, E-I-E-I-O
With a quack quack here, and a quack quack there,
Here a quack there a quack everywhere a quack
With a chick chick here, and a chick chick there,
Here a chick there a chick everywhere a chick chick
Old Macdonald had a farm E-I-E-I-O.

Old Macdonald had a farm, E-I-E-I-O,
And on this farm he had some turkeys, E-I-E-I-O
With a gobble gobble here, and a gobble gobble there,
Here a gobble there a gobble everywhere a gobble
With a quack quack here, and a quack quack there,
Here a quack there a quack everywhere a quack
With a chick chick here, and a chick chick there,
Here a chick there a chick everywhere a chick chick
Old Macdonald had a farm E-I-E-I-O.

Old Macdonald had a farm, E-I-E-I-O,
And on this farm he had some cows, E-I-E-I-O
With a moo moo here, and a moo moo there,
Here a moo there a moo everywhere a moo
With a gobble gobble here, and a gobble gobble there,
Here a gobble there a gobble everywhere a gobble
With a quack quack here, and a quack quack there,
Here a quack there a quack everywhere a quack
With a chick chick here, and a chick chick there,
Here a chick there a chick everywhere a chick chick
Old Macdonald had a farm E-I-E-I-O.
```

Note finally

(a) The standard end of line and end of file functions ('eoln' and 'eof')
refer to the default file 'input' unless a file name is specified as in
this program (for example, 'eoln(farmyard)').

(b) The advantage of placing the data for this program in a file is that
we can now change the animal names and noises to print out a
variety of different verses without program alteration. A general
rule in computing is that it is always easier to make changes to
data than to a program.

12.3   Word processing

As the invention of computers brought automatic data processing
into the world of the clerk so the decreasing cost and size of today's
computers has brought the 'word processor' into the secretarial world.
Office administration revolves traditionally around mountains of paper-

work: the production and dispatch of letters, memoranda, invoices, advertising literature, filing, and so on. Virtually all these activities focus on the processing of text in one form or another and it is this activity at which the computer is particularly good.

One of the important requirements of a word processing system is the ability to support the rapid production and correction of correspondence. Flexible input and editing programs are used to produce a copy of a letter, for example, in a file which can be displayed on a VDU for proofreading and correction. Only when the letter is approved for sending is it actually printed on paper using a high-quality printer (or, where it is available, transmitted electronically to the recipient's word processing system). A facility that is usually included in these systems to provide neat layout of text is *justification*: the lines of a document are adjusted as in printed texts to achieve a uniformly sized right margin whenever possible. An example of text justifying is shown in figure 12.4.

Figure 12.4. Text justification.

```
In reply to your letter of the 12th January 1982, I am pleased to
advise that the goods referred to in our invoice no. 123456
have indeed been dispatched to your address yesterday.
We must apologise most sincerely for the delay in sending out your
Super Blaster Mark 6 Minimegamicrowongerbox ordered
last March, but trust that you will appreciate that the delay
was due to circumstances entirely beyond
our control.
```

a) Paragraph as typed

```
In  reply  to  your  letter  of  the 12th January 1982, I am
pleased  to advise that the goods referred to in our invoice
no.  123456  have  indeed  been  dispatched  to your address
yesterday.  We must  apologise most sincerely for the delay
in sending out your Super Blaster Mark 6 Minimegamicrowonge-
rbox  ordered last March, but trust that you will appreciate
that  the delay was due to circumstances entirely beyond our
control.
```

b) Paragraph after justification

In the example below, a paragraph of text is read from a file and printed in justified format.

Example 12.2

Read and justify a paragraph of text.

The first thing to note in this problem is that the format of the text in the input file is irrelevant. For example, it does not matter how long the lines of text in the source may be, since the justifying program must ignore end of lines and produce a new, clean layout with lines that are, as far as possible, of equal length. Similarly, since new spacing will be created, it is unimportant how many spaces occur between words in the source: one or many will produce the same result. There are two main parts to this task:

> **repeat**
>   read sufficient text for one output line
>   justify and print the line
> **until** end of file

Firstly, we must decide on a line length for the printed text and devise a data structure in which to place this line. In a complete word processing system the line length would be variable to permit the production of documents of varying dimensions but in our case we shall define the line length as a constant in the program:

> **const** linelength = 60   {an arbitrary choice}

The line is conveniently stored in an array:

> **var** buffer:**array** [1..linelength] **of** char;

The first thorny problem concerns how we decide where to end a line in the justified text. We wish to avoid splitting words between lines if at all possible and so we shall use the following algorithm:

1. Fill 'buffer' with characters from the input file, discarding newlines and surplus spaces.
2. Find the end of the last complete word in 'buffer'.
3. Justify and print the line up to and including this word.

A consequence of effectively shortening the line by backing up to the end of the last complete word is that we shall have some left-over text at the end which must be carried over to the following line. It is also necessary to cater for the possibility of finding a very long word at the end of 'buffer' – in the extreme case 'buffer' may be all one word, for example,

> aaaaaaaaaaaaaaaaaaaaaaaaaaaaaaarrrrrrrrrrrrrrrrrrrrrrrrrrrrrrrgh!

– in which case we must resort to splitting the word and inserting a hyphen at the end of the current line. Deciding when to split a word is open to debate but we shall adopt the policy of splitting the last word in 'buffer' if no space is found within 15 characters back from the end of 'buffer'; that is, if the last word is 15 characters or more long.

A reasonable way of saving the tail-end of a line is to use a second array:

> **var** tail:**array** [1 . . taillength] **of** char;

into which we can copy the text left over. From the above we deduce that the longest possible tail will be 15 characters, though by declaring 'taillength' as a constant we retain the flexibility to change fairly easily the criterion for word splitting.

The routine to read characters into 'buffer' needs to discard extra spaces beyond the single space separating words. This is a good application for a Boolean flag to be used to mark the reading of a space so that we may ignore any following ones. Also, since words in the input stream may be separated by the end of a line boundary rather than a space we must ensure that only a single separating space remains in this case. In practice, this is easy to handle since the character read at the end of a line (that is, when 'eoln(infile)' is 'true') is indeed a space. We simply ignore the line structure of 'infile' and continue to read characters one by one.

Using an integer 'ptr' to index the array, a suitable sequence of statements for reading a complete buffer from the file 'infile' is

```
ptr:= 1;
lastisspace:= true;   {the Boolean flag}
repeat
  read(infile,buffer[ptr]);
  if buffer[ptr] < > space
    then begin lastisspace:= false; ptr:= ptr+1 end
    else if not lastisspace
         then begin lastisspace:= true; ptr:= ptr+1 end
until eof(infile) or (ptr > linelength)
```

'lastisspace' is initialised to 'true', here, since the first character read into 'buffer' is assumed to be the first of a new word. The end of file case is special in that the very last line should not be justified at all. To do so could stretch a short line across the page artificially. In the second part of the algorithm we attempt to locate the end of the last complete word in 'buffer', except in the end of file case:

> **if** eof(infile)
>   **then** fill out line with spaces

```
    else begin
            find end of line position in 'buffer'
            if a word is to be split
                then insert hyphen
            else begin
                    copy remaining characters to 'tail'
                    justify the text in 'buffer'
                end
        end
```

Finding the end of line position in 'buffer' involves looking at the characters backward from the end to see if a space is encountered before 15 characters ('taillength') have been examined. There are two criteria for deciding whether to split a word. Firstly, if there is no space within the 'taillength' characters of the end of 'buffer' then a hyphen will be inserted at the end of 'buffer', displacing the last character which becomes the 'tail' copied over to the next buffer. The other case occurs when a space is found in the above scan but the remaining text is all one word, meaning that there are no spaces that can be expanded to justify the line. The buffer is processed in the same way in either of these events. We may expand 'if a word is to be split' to:

```
        calculate 'spacecount' = number of spaces in 'buffer' (excluding
            tail)
        if length of tail > = 'taillength' or spacecount is zero
            then ... .
```

The method we shall adopt for justifying the text in the constructed line is relatively crude. Having removed a number of characters (the tail) from the line we now insert the same number of characters in the form of extra spaces distributed as evenly as possible between the words on the line. If the number of new spaces is held in 'spaces' then the process of justification becomes:

```
        calculate 'new space size' = 'spaces' div 'spacecount'
        calculate 'additional spaces' = 'spaces' mod 'spacecount'
        replace each space in 'buffer' by a space + 'new space size'
            spaces, also adding in the additional spaces.
```

An example should make this clearer. Suppose on entry to this part of the program that there are 12 words (11 spaces) in 'buffer' and that it has been established that an extra 14 spaces must be added to justify the line.

We must replace each of the 11 spaces by a space plus 'new space size' spaces (= 14 **div** 11, i.e. 1), giving two spaces between each word. This still leaves us 3 (14 **mod** 11) spaces short in line length. These additional spaces are added, one at a time, to the first three sets of spaces between words giving the following skeleton structure for the line, where '—' stands for a word and 's' for a space.

left   right

margin   margin

$$|\text{—3s—3s—3s—2s—2s—2s—2s—2s—2s—2s—2s—}|$$

The final part of the algorithm entails printing out the justified line, copying the truncated tail to the start of 'buffer' and reading further characters by looping back to the start. The full program is quite long but follows from the above discussion sufficiently directly to make further elaboration unnecessary. Note that the process of inserting extra spaces into a line occurs twice and requires characters to be shifted to the right in order to make room. It is written as a procedure which takes the number of spaces to be inserted as a parameter.

In the complete program in figure 12.5, 'tlen' represents the length of the tail of a line and procedure 'insert' is used to insert new spaces in a line.

Figure 12.5. The text justification program.

```
program justify (infile,output);

const linelength = 60;
      taillength = 15;
      space = ' '; hyphen = '-';

var buffer : array [1..linelength] of char;
    tail : array [1..taillength] of char;
    ptr,tptr,tlen,spacecount,newspacesize,
     extras,spaces : integer;
    lastisspace : boolean;
    infile : text;

procedure insert (spno : integer);
{insert 'spno' spaces at position 'ptr' in the buffer}
var sptr,count,top : integer;

begin
 top := linelength - spno;
 {move characters along in 'buffer' to make room}
 for sptr := top downto ptr do
  buffer[sptr+spno] := buffer[sptr];
  {insert 'spno' spaces}
  for count := 1 to spno do
   begin ptr := ptr+1; buffer[ptr] := space end
end;
```

```
begin {main program}
 reset(infile,'sample'); {connects 'infile' to the external file
                          'sample'}
ptr := 1;
lastisspace := true;
repeat
  {read a buffer full, reducing multiple spaces to one}
  repeat
   read(infile,buffer[ptr]);
   if buffer[ptr] <> space
    then begin lastisspace := false; ptr := ptr+1 end
    else if not lastisspace
            then begin lastisspace := true; ptr := ptr+1 end
  until eof(infile) or (ptr > linelength);

  if eof(infile)
   then {fill out line with spaces}
    while ptr <= linelength do
     begin buffer[ptr] := space; ptr := ptr+1 end
   else begin {find tail}
        ptr := linelength;

        {find last space in buffer}
        while (buffer[ptr]<>space) and
              (ptr>linelength-taillength) do
         ptr := ptr-1;
        {calculate length of tail}
        tlen := linelength-ptr;
        {count spaces up to tail}
        spacecount := 0;
        for ptr := 1 to linelength-tlen-1 do
         if buffer[ptr] = space
          then spacecount := spacecount + 1;
        {save tail}
        if (tlen>=taillength) or (spacecount=0)
         then begin {word must be split}
              tail[1] := buffer[linelength];
              buffer[linelength] := hyphen;
              tlen := 1
              end
         else begin {copy tail and justify}
              for tptr := 1 to tlen do
               tail[tptr] := buffer[linelength-tlen+tptr];
              spaces := tlen + 1;
              {calculate new space sizes}
              newspacesize := spaces div spacecount;
              {and remaining extra spaces}
              extras := spaces mod spacecount;
              {now add spaces to justify}
              ptr := 1;
              repeat
               if buffer[ptr] = space
                then begin
                     if extras > 0
                      then begin
                           insert(newspacesize+1);
                           extras := extras-1
                           end
                      else insert(newspacesize)
                     end;
```

```
                    ptr := ptr+1
                until (ptr>linelength) or
                        ((newspacesize=0) and (extras=0))
            end
        end;

    {print line}
    for ptr := 1 to linelength do write(buffer[ptr]);
    writeln;

    if not eof(infile)
      then begin {copy tail to start of buffer}
            ptr := 1;
            for tptr := 1 to tlen do
              begin buffer[ptr] := tail[tptr]; ptr := ptr+1 end
          end

    until eof(infile)

end.
```

In practice, many word processing quality printers permit a sophisticated modification of print density along a line by using a series of fine horizontal increments to position the print head before each character is printed. Proportional spacing, as this facility is called, allows justification to be performed by stretching or compressing the width of all characters in small increments, giving a smooth quality to the text.

12.4   Grammatical analysis

The grammar of a language is the set of rules that make it possible to ascertain which sentences are legal in that language and which are not. Grammar is of interest to linguists in their quest for a better understanding of natural languages but it is also of considerable importance to computer scientists. After all, one of the main tasks of a Pascal compiler is to verify that a user's program conforms to the syntax, or grammatical structure, of the Pascal language and to inform the user of any failure to adhere to this grammar.

A principal difference between the task of the linguist and that of the computer scientist, however, is that whereas the programming language Pascal can be proved to possess an unambiguous, well-defined grammar of limited complexity, no complete, similarly rigorous grammar for English is known to exist. Even relatively limited attempts to devise algorithmic grammatical rules for a natural language quickly become complex and ridden with special cases. This is not the place to delve too deeply into this dichotomy but a couple of examples are given below to illustrate the gravity of the problem of analysing natural languages.

Perhaps the most well-known attempt to provide a set of grammatical rules for English is N. Chomsky's *Transformational Grammar* (MIT Press, Cambridge, Mass., 1965) in which a large set of transformations is postulated to convert phrases to and from more basic forms. Though a powerful tool in the hands of an experienced human user, it was quickly realised that TG was not at all easy to implement on a computer, largely because of the frequent difficulty in deciding which transforms to apply and when to apply them.

Consider the case of a transformation that may be applied to the utterance

> I never met a man who is taller than John

This may be transformed into

> I never met a taller man than John

in appropriate circumstances. Unfortunately, determining 'appropriate circumstances' involves a knowledge that 'John' is a man, since we would not entertain the same transformation on 'I never met a man who was taller than Maria'. The decision on this can be very difficult: we can only prevent application of the transform on 'I never met a man who was taller than George Eliot', for example, by including our non-linguistic knowledge that George Eliot was a woman. The crux of the matter is that only superficial analysis of English is possible based on syntax alone. A second example brings this home very strongly:

> The soldiers fired at the women and I saw several of them fall
> (Y. Wilks, 1973)

Any sensible algorithm for interpreting the meaning of this sentence must be able to work out to whom the 'them' refers. *We* know that 'them' refers almost certainly to the women rather than the soldiers but our train of thought in arriving at this conclusion is complex from an automaton's viewpoint. Put pedantically it may go something like 'soldiers use tools which expel projectiles and people who are hit by such projectiles have a greater propensity to fall down than those who propel them'. Behind these two examples lie a depth of real-world experience which computer scientists are striving, with at present only limited success, to model.

On a more practical level, the identification of the constituent elements of a statement in an artificial language (called 'parsing' in keeping with natural language terminology) is an essential requirement in compiling a program and in many other applications. We owe to Chomsky, again, a neat system of classification of grammatical types, the simplest of which is referred to by computer scientists as a 'finite-state' grammar. This is far removed from the complex structures required in a natural language but we may use finite-state grammars to describe simple formats.

Suppose, for example, that we wish to read a series of initials and surnames of people and set out by describing the form of such names as follows:

> A surname consists of one or more upper-case alphabetic characters preceded by a space and terminated by a comma. An optional number of initials terminated by full stops may precede the surname.

Thus,

> K.H. BENNETT,
> M.J.K. SMITH,
>   WHITE,   (note preceding space)

are examples of names under this definition. A rigidly defined format such as this could be useful, for example, in checking for errors in entering names into the computer.

An immediate problem shown in even this simple example is that such definitions, made in English, are at best long-winded and at worst

Figure 12.6. A finite-state grammar.

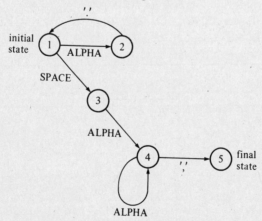

ambiguous. One way of tightening up the definition is to recognise that what is being described here is in essence a very basic grammar of a simple language in which all 'sentences' are names. This may seem odd, but it allows us to recast the rules as a finite-state grammar as shown in figure 12.6.

At any point in the processing of a potential name there is the concept of the current *state* of the machine, initially state 1. States are numbered 1 to 5 and enclosed in circles in figure 12.6. Analysis proceeds with the reading of a prospective name character by character and with transitions from state to state depending on the values or types of characters. If the first character read is alphabetic, for example, the state changes from 1 to 2 as shown and the next character is considered. In this case we would expect a full stop in a correct name, indicating a transition back into state 1. Eventually, we expect to find a space in the name which will take us to state 3 followed by one or more alphabetic characters forcing a transition from state 3 to state 4 and then repeated transitions from state 4 to state 4 again. Only on encountering a comma do we enter the final state, state 5, and this last transition heralds the successful identification of a name by our definition.

Along the way it is quite possible that a character may be encountered for which a path is not shown. All such cases represent an error in the formatting of the name and are easily detected. The definition of a name is now unambiguously represented by this finite-state grammar. Furthermore, the progress of an attempt to check the format of a name is uniquely described at any stage by (1) the current state and (2) the next input character, which makes it particularly straightforward to implement the technique algorithmically. To do this we first convert the finite-state diagram of figure 12.6 into the finite-state table shown in figure 12.7.

The finite-state table displays the transitions to make for any combination of current state and next character encountered. For example, when in

Figure 12.7. Finite-state table.

		next character				
		ALPHA	.	SPACE	,	
	1	2	E	3	E	
current	2	E	1	E	E	
state	3	4	E	E	E	
	4	4	E	E	5	E = error

state 1, if the next character is a space, state 3 is entered. Note that encountering a comma whilst in state 4 will be identified as a successful terminating condition (state 5); we have no need for a fifth row in the table.

In a program, we can use a two-dimensional integer array to hold a state table, representing the error states by, say, '−1'.

> **const** states = 4; inputs = 4;
> **var** stab:**array** [1..states,1..inputs] **of** integer;

The outline of a program to check the format of a name can now be drawn up:

> **program** parsename (input,statefile,output);
> **begin**
>   read state table values from a file
>   initialise 'state' to 1
>   **repeat**
>   read the next character in the prospective name
>   determine the type of this character
>   make a state transition if no error is detected
>   **until** (state = 5) **or** error detected
>   output result
> **end**.

The result of this simple program is a message confirming that the name conforms to the defined syntax or that it does not. The 'type' of a character referred to in this design is in fact the column index in the state table; type 1 is any (upper-case) alphabetic character, type 2 = '.' and so on. An error will be detected if the character does not fit into any of these types. Providing no error has been detected a state transition is made by retrieving the new state from the state table array (stab) indexed by the current state and the character type. By far the most flexible and convenient way of initialising the state table array is to read the table values from a file containing the following data:

2	−1	3	−1
−1	1	−1	−1
4	−1	−1	−1
4	−1	−1	5

The complete program is given in figure 12.8.

Figure 12.8. The name parsing program.

```
program parsename (input,statefile,output);

const states=4; inputs=4; fullstop='.';
     space=' '; comma=',';

var stab : array [1..states,1..inputs] of integer;
    ch : char;
    error : boolean;
    chartype,state : integer;
    statefile : text;

begin
 reset(statefile,'states');{connects'statefile' to the external
                          file 'states'}
 {read state table}
 for state := 1 to states do
  for chartype := 1 to inputs do
   read(statefile,stab[state,chartype]);

 {initialise}
 state := 1; error := false;

 repeat
  read(ch);
  {determine char type}
  if ch in ['A'..'Z']
   then chartype := 1
   else if ch = fullstop
          then chartype := 2
          else if ch = space
                 then chartype := 3
                 else if ch = comma
                        then chartype := 4
                        else error := true;

  if not error
   then begin {make state transition}
          state := stab[state,chartype];
          if state = -1 then error := true;
        end

 until (state = 5) or error;

 if error
  then write('Name wrongly formatted')
  else write('Name OK.')

end.
```

It is interesting to note that the above program is an example of an algorithm that is said to be 'table driven'. In other words it is possible to change the algorithm by changing the contents of the table and this in turn can be achieved by changing the contents of the data file 'statefile'. For example, we could allow any number of spaces between initials and surname simply by replacing the error state in row 3 column 3 of the table by a 3, indicating a reentry to state 3 on encountering further spaces at this point. Note, however, that only state transitions can be modified by this technique. It is not possible to revise the classes of input characters without rewriting the relevant program statements.

In conclusion, a word of caution: there are many problems which are potentially suitable for solution by a finite-state grammar approach but which may be solved more easily using a more powerful grammar. The number of states required to formulate a finite-state grammar rises very rapidly with increasing complexity of the 'language' being defined.

Exercises

12.1 Write a program to list the frequency of occurrence of all (upper-case) letters in a file containing text.

As a more advanced problem, sort the list to print the letters in descending order of frequency and apply the program to as long a file of normal text as practicable. If you have a file of encoded text from exercise 11.5, apply the program to this file and try to 'crack the code' using the two sorted lists.

12.2 Rule a grid of, say, 8 × 8 squares and draw a picture or shape by filling squares with various characters (most may be left blank if desired). Input the rows of characters to a file, each row on a separate line, and write a program to read the grid and print out the mirror image of the shape. Now print out the mirror image upside-down!

12.3 One of the simplest and most reliable tests for automatically discriminating between authors is to establish the relative frequency with which they make use of specific function words (for example, 'upon', 'by' or 'too'). Write a program that will read in a list of up to ten such words and count and display the frequency (occurrences per thousand words) of each of these function words in a file containing a passage of text.

12.4 Using a finite-state grammar or otherwise, write a program to check for errors in the syntax of postcodes which have the following syntax:

1 or more upper-case letters followed by
1 or more digits followed by
1 space followed by
1 digit followed by
2 upper-case letters

Analysing data and presenting results

This chapter is concerned mainly with applications involving the collection, input and processing of data from observational sources (experiments, questionnaires, field observations, etc.) and with techniques of presenting the results. The important Pascal feature 'record' is also introduced.

The use of computers to assimilate, analyse and present results from data acquired in the course of observational and experimental studies has increased steadily in the wake of more generally available and cheaper computing facilities. This increase is sustained by a realisation that sizeable volumes of data can now be generated by such studies in the knowledge that subsequent analysis will no longer entail months of painstaking hand calculation of results. The sources of such data are numerous, ranging from scientific apparatus to bee behaviour; from chemical reactions to opinion polls.

In practice, despite the apparent diversity of sources of data, many of these applications exhibit considerable similarities when examined from the viewpoint of data acquisition, analysis and presentation of results. For example, in the field of event recording it matters little to a computer whether the types and timing of events were recorded by scientists in a laboratory or by an ornithologist in the field. The algorithms used to search for significant features in both these sets of data could well be identical. On the other hand, there are some significant differences between sources of data as well as similarities. We shall try to give some degree of feel for these below and for some of the pitfalls in this kind of processing.

An introduction to techniques of data analysis would be incomplete, however, without mention of special programs or 'packages' available to users. Though not necessarily directly associated with Pascal, the availability of a suitable package should be one of the first considerations.

13.1 Packages

A *package* is a complete program or suite of programs that presents a set of standard facilities to users in the form of a self-contained unit with operating instructions. The intention is that, with the assistance of a reference manual, a user may apply certain standard algorithms to data in a specified format (usually held in a file), without having to write these algorithms in the first place. The most widely used packages are those containing statistical algorithms.

Sometimes, standard routines are provided as 'library' procedures rather than as self-contained packages, requiring at least a short user program to set up the input data as parameters, to call the library procedures and to make appropriate use of the returned results. This approach is most commonly used for numerical and graphics routines, where the procedure calls form only a part of the total processing required. Bear in mind that if the facility is available, access to any externally defined programs or procedures falls outside the present ISO Pascal standard and will require reference to local documentation.

Packages are certainly very powerful tools. Without them users would be faced with the unenviable task of 're-inventing the wheel' each time a common routine is required. Furthermore, even simple statistical algorithms, for example, require very careful implementation on a computer to make them reliable and efficient. Though one has the initial, occasionally daunting, task of mastering the operating instructions there is little excuse for re-writing programs that are available in suitable form in a package.

Unfortunately, things are never quite as simple as they sound. As well as being very powerful tools packages are also potentially very dangerous ones. Their danger stems from the very fact that they are so easy to use and demand only minimal knowledge of their contents to produce results. The temptation is to apply ever more complex algorithms to data simply because they are available rather than because they are suitable. The moral is never to use a package routine without a clear understanding of the inherent assumptions and limitations.

Closely allied to this point is the question of the accuracy of any given result from a package, particularly where 'real' arithmetic is involved. Misuse of a numerical analysis or statistical routine, for example, could easily result in an answer of apparently great precision being in fact dominated by a series of accumulated arithmetic errors which are unlikely to be reported automatically.

A more general limitation of a package is that it is almost certainly written to allow widest possible use in a number of different applications and may constrain the user into supplying the data in a very rigid format. Normally, this will not cause serious problems unless the data have been collected prior to studying the required format and are found later to contain variables that are incompatible with the stated conventions. In such circumstances it is usually, though not always, possible to transform the data into suitable format by writing a conversion program.

The output from a package may appear in many different forms. Depending on the application this will vary from a single value or set of values to tabular or graphical output. However, it is usually possible to arrange for the output to be sent to a file for further processing by another program if desired.

A couple of questions to ask yourself (and, if possible, a sympathetic experienced user) *before* any data are collected may be summarised as follows:

(a) Is the task feasible? Though the computer and software package will fill in the details, work out roughly the processing required to analyse your data, using the package manual as a guide. In a statistics package, for example, are there too many variables to handle, or are there so many complicated relationships that 'combinatorial explosion' will prevent a complete analysis within the allowable resources? In a numerical routine, is the precision of real numbers adequate to give a result of the desired accuracy?

(b) What is the most convenient format for the data? There are two sides to this question. On the one hand, the package manual will specify exactly how the data are to be presented and how the user is to inform the package of this format. Such mechanisms are invariably designed for maximum computing convenience but not necessarily with user 'friendliness' in mind. On the other hand, the gatherer of the data will have better things to do than to write down long and precisely positioned strings of digits or characters for the mere convenience of a machine. This apparent dilemma is resolved if a special program is written to accept data from the user in a 'human' form and to generate a file in the format required by the package. Not only is this more convenient to the user it is also considerably more reliable and we shall discuss the writing of such programs later in this chapter.

13.2   Files, records and fields

When considering the processing of data that are in the form of perhaps a large number of related sets of values it is useful to describe the structure of the data in terms of a file made up of *records* and *fields*.

A *record* in this sense is a single set of values, not necessarily of the same data type, that are in some way related. For example, in a study to observe spawning behaviour in trout we could create a record for each trout examined, as shown in figure 13.1(*a*).

Each item within a record is called a *field*; for example, the 'length' field or 'date' field in this example. It is good practice, regardless of the area of study, to design at the outset a coding manual for your data which contains a definitive explanation of the structure and permitted ranges of values of all fields in a record. The coding manual is then available as a reference document when creating and entering records into a file and, most importantly, it will serve as a reminder during subsequent analysis. Readers with long-term memories which are as bad as the author's will quickly appreciate the value of such documentation when working on projects lasting several months or years!

The importance of careful design of a coding format in survey analysis cannot be overstressed. The nature of data to collect, the level of detail most

Figure 13.1. Input data structure.

species	date	location	length(in)	weight(lb)	spawn
R	20/10/81	A6	23	4·2	F
R	31/10/81	B3	11	0·9	I
B	28/11/81	A8	19	3·7	S

(*a*) Sample records

species

R   Rainbow
B   Brown
A   American Brook
G   Grayling
O   Other

location

Grid reference, from survey map
Horizontal code (letter) first.

spawn : spawning status

T   Trace spawn
F   Full spawn
S   Spawned
I   Immature
N   No trace
O   Other

(*b*) Coding manual extract

appropriate and the most suitable way in which to express a field are vital considerations to make before data are collected. It is relatively easy to make even drastic changes to data formats and choice of fields at the coding manual design stage but usually difficult and sometimes impossible to make small changes after some or all of the data are collected. Some general points to note are:

1. Records and fields within records may be of fixed or variable length. For example, a field containing a person's surname may be defined as variable length and adjusted to fit exactly the number of characters required or it may be fixed at, say, 20 characters long. Truncation of longer names and filling out of shorter names with spaces would occur in the latter case. In general, although variable length fields may allow greater input flexibility and may save space if most entries are relatively short, it is usually more difficult to process data in variable length fields and few packages will accept them.

2. Related to the above storage methods, the actual input of data may be in free- or fixed-format. In fixed-format input each data field is allocated a fixed column or set of column positions in the record being entered and the fields are identifiable by this physical position. Data entered in free-format, that is, not tied to specific column positions, are recognised by delimiters (for example, spaces) separating the fields.

3. The practice of abbreviating classes of data as shown in the above example (for example, species as 'R', 'B', 'A', 'G', or 'O') certainly reduces the amount of coding required and increases the speed of entry. Too much abbreviation, however, may be counter-productive, if the shortened codes are too numerous or complex to remember without looking them up.

13.3   Pascal records

The record defined in figure 13.1 contains eight fields (counting the date as three fields) which hold values of the following data types:

species	– char	length	– integer
day, month, year	– integer	weight	– real
location	– 2 chars	spawn	– char

Since a single record is a coherent entity in its own right it would seem useful to imagine a data type called, say, 'fishrecords' of which each record is a member, and to be able to assign a selected record to a special variable of type 'fishrecords'. In other words, we would be able to refer to a complete single record within a Pascal program by means of an identifier of type 'fishrecords'.

We cannot use an array to group fields within one record because elements of an array must be of exactly the same type, a requirement that is not satisfied in the trout survey example.

A **record** data type for the above example may be defined in Pascal as follows:

```
type fishrecords = record
                species:char;
                day,month,year:integer;
                locycoord,locxcoord:char;
                length:integer;
                weight:real;
                spawn:char
            end
```

Like an array, a **record** is a structured data object containing a number of components. Unlike an array, the components may be of different types and, as shown below, items are accessed by name, not by subscript.

Variables of type 'fishrecords' may be declared:

```
var oneitem:fishrecords;
```

and to select a given field within the structured variable 'oneitem' we use a full stop as a field *selector*, as in

```
oneitem.day   {identifies the 'day' field of the record}
```

The identifier 'oneitem.day' can be used in any of the ways in which a simple integer identifier would be appropriate; for example, in assignment or printing:

```
oneitem.day:= 30
```
or
```
write(oneitem.day)
```

Using a **record** definition in this way provides a means of carrying the design of an input record into the Pascal program itself, with all the benefits of clarity and self-documentation that this implies. Interrelated values are gathered together under a single name in a consistent manner.

13.4   Entry and verification of data

Until quite recently, the preparation of data for entry into a computer usually involved an 'offline' medium, that is, the production of a machine-readable copy of the data using special data processing equipment which is not connected to the computer. Punched cards were a particularly common offline medium. Data in this form were then fed into the computer as a complete batch for storage or direct processing. The arrival in numbers of the visual display unit marked a move towards direct ('online') keyboard entry of data into the computer filestore without the need for an intermediate machine-readable form.

Though the end product of both of these routes is the same (a computer file of data) direct entry offers two attractive additional facilities:

1. Strong visual prompts can be given from a special input program to guide the user through the input process.
2. Values can be checked for obvious mistakes immediately they are entered and the user informed of definite or potential errors.

When entering large volumes of data these are both useful techniques to employ. A suitable prompt may vary from the simple expedient of displaying the next field name on the VDU screen to a comprehensive 'menu' display of possible options as illustrated in figure 13.2.

Which approach to use depends on a number of factors, including the complexity of the coding manual, the nature of the document from which data are being transcribed and the familiarity of the keyboard operator with the subject material. A menu style of presentation or excessively long prompting should be avoided if the VDU is unable to display the material very rapidly since the user will soon become bored with having to wait more than a fraction of a second for the next prompt to finish.

In the above scheme, data are entered under the control of a special input program written by the user and tailored to the application in hand. If this technique is used, the second advantage – that of being able to check the entered values – becomes possible. Some of the simplest verifying techniques are given below:

Figure 13.2. Menu display.

Species field

R	Rainbow	A	American Brook	O	Other
B	Brown	G	Grayling		

Select species: ____

(a) *Set membership*

Responses to values requested for certain fields such as the 'species' field above are severely limited and can be checked against a list of acceptable values. An illegal response should result in a suitable warning message followed by a 'try again' prompt. A common ploy is to include a 'bell' character in the output message which sounds the bleeper present in many VDU terminals to alert the user to an immediate problem. If the character set of your computer is ASCII the statement 'write(chr(7))' should achieve this (using the standard function 'chr' to form the 'bell' character from its numerical code).

(b) *Range checking*

Many numeric values are known to be limited in range, as is the case of the date fields of 'fishrecords'. A simple check will ensure that no 'month' entry lies outside the range 1 to 12, for example.

(c) *Double entry*

Particularly crucial fields in a record may justify the inclusion of a double entry condition which obliges the keyboard operator to type a value twice. The two values can be compared in the checking program and not accepted unless they are the same. Note that to be most effective the repeat entry of a value should not occur immediately after the first. Better to return to the double entry fields at the end of entering a complete record to minimise the chance of duplicating an erroneous response.

Other techniques may be employed during this interactive input phase. In entering people's names as strings of characters, for example, the computer may be programmed to fill out a short name with spaces to a fixed length. The most common values expected in particular fields may be defined in advance and entered automatically if the '**return**' key alone is pressed. These are called default entries and a good interactive system will display relevant default values alongside the prompts for data entry. On completion of a batch of entries the same program, or another, could be used to look through the file for identical records indicating a possible duplication – this is often made easier by first sorting the records in the file so that identical records will lie side by side. Many computer systems provide a 'sort package' which will do this re-ordering without the need to write a special sort program.

13.5 Presenting results

Too often the output from a data analysis program or package is presented to the user in an indigestible format making interpretation of the results difficult. It may be relatively easy to request a package to provide pages and pages of statistical tables, for example, but far less easy for us mere mortals to make any sense of them. The basic goal is to obtain more information from less data, and not vice versa.

When using packages one may have little say in how the results are to be presented but it is sometimes possible to write a post-processing program to reformat output or, indeed, to carry out further analysis not directly available in the package. Sometimes, a graphical display of results can convey more information to the eye than a tabular listing and, in the absence of a friendly package routine, it is not usually too difficult to devise a fairly general program to present tabular data pictorially.

The example chosen below produces a histogram chart as an alternative to a table of frequency distributions. The histogram may be printed on a conventional printer (for example, a line printer) which has the characteristic that the chart must be printed one line at a time to give a picture like that in figure 13.4.

Example 13.1

Display a frequency distribution of n variables as a histogram with automatic scaling.

To keep the program as flexible as possible we shall arrange for values of the variables (vertical, or y-axis) to be scaled automatically. Also, the width of blocks on the horizontal (x-) axis will be adjusted to suit the number of variables being displayed. A limit is imposed in the latter case by the maximum width of the page on which we are printing. Similarly, if the output is to be printed within the confines of a page as, for example, between paper perforations on a line printer, then the y-axis scaling is determined by the available number of lines per page.

With these characteristics in mind an initial level of description for the problem solution is attempted:

> Read the number of variables to display and their values
> Calculate horizontal and vertical axis scales
> Plot histogram

Because we need to refer continually to the variable values they will be read into an array which must be large enough to hold the largest number of variables we can handle. Let us call this 'maxvars' and impose a value of 60, which is the most variables that could be displayed across a typical page width. The array is

> **var** histodata : **array** [1 . . maxvars] **of** real;

In practice, we will not use all elements of 'histodata' in a plot where 'n' is less than 'maxvars'. Reading the number of variables and their values is straightforward:

> read(n);
> **for** index : = 1 **to** n **do** read(histodata[index])

though it may be desirable to modify this to read the values directly from a different text file to 'input'.

Perhaps the trickiest part of the whole problem is to calculate the vertical scale for the plot. One of the simplest techniques is to make the limit of the scale the nearest power of ten above the largest value: for example, to run the scale from 0 to 100 if the largest of the values is 67. To find the limit we must first find the largest value:

> ymax : = histodata[1];
> **for** index : = 2 **to** n **do**
>   **if** histodata[index] > ymax **then** ymax : = histodata[index]

and repeatedly divide this by 10 to find the limit:

> ylimit : = 1;
> **while** ymax > = 1 **do**
>   **begin**
>   ymax : = ymax/10;
>   ylimit : = ylimit*10
>   **end**

The number of character positions used per variable on the horizontal scale is easier to determine. Given 'pagewidth', a **const** set at the program start to the total number of print positions across the page:

> xinterval : = (pagewidth − 10) **div** n

using integer variables and leaving some space for the vertical axis and its interval markings.

The final part of the scaling is to choose a vertical scale resolution. For simplicity, if we choose 50 lines as the vertical scale this will allow us to plot the histogram values with a resolution of 2% of the full scale value and to fit the whole plot onto a typical printer page length (between perforations) of 60–70 lines. Thus,

> yinterval: = ylimit/50

Actually, we are also interested in half this resolution, to use in finding the nearest vertical scale positions corresponding to the values of the variables, that is, for a given vertical scale value 'yposn' we shall print a line if

> value > yposn − yinterval/2

The rest of the program (figure 13.3) is concerned largely with the detailed positioning of characters on the page, especially the vertical and horizontal axes and their markings. Note that the output of this program is sent to *output* and hence, normally, to the VDU screen. It will be necessary to redirect the output as described in local documentation in order to print the histogram on a printer.

Figure 13.3. The histogram program.

```pascal
program histoplot (input,output);

const pagewidth = 132; {line printer size}
      maxvars = 60;      {greatest number of variables}

var histodata : array [1..maxvars] of real;
    ylimit, lines, index, xinterval, xposn, n, i : integer;
    ymax, yinterval, yposn : real;

begin
 {read variables}
 read(n);
 for index := 1 to n do read(histodata[index]);

 {set vertical scale size}
 ymax := histodata[1];
 for index := 2 to n do
  if histodata[index] > ymax then ymax := histodata[index];
 ylimit:=1;
 while ymax >= 1 do
  begin
   ymax := ymax / 10;
   ylimit := ylimit * 10
  end;
 yinterval := ylimit / 50:
```

```
{set horizontal scale size}
xinterval := (pagewidth - 10) div n;

{print histogram}
writeln;
yposn := ylimit;
for lines := 50 downto 1 do
  begin
    {draw vertical axis mark}
    if lines mod 5 = 0
    then write(yposn:8:0,' -')
    else write(' ':9,'!');

    {print spaces or asterisks for this line}
    for xposn := 1 to n do
      if histodata[xposn] > yposn - yinterval / 2
        then for i := 1 to xinterval do write('*')
        else write(' ':xinterval);

    {set up for next line}
    writeln;
    yposn := yposn - yinterval
  end;
```

Figure 13.4. Output from the histogram program.

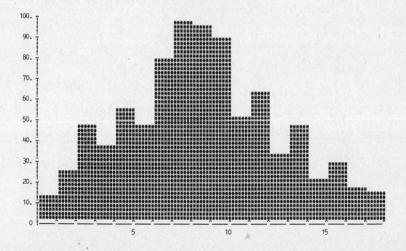

```
{draw horizontal axis}
write(0:8,' !');
for xposn := 1 to n do
 begin
  for i := 1 to xinterval - 1 do write('-');
  write('^')
 end;
writeln; writeln; write(' ':10);
for xposn := 1 to n do
 if xposn mod 5 = 0
   then write(xposn:xinterval)
   else write(' ':xinterval);
writeln; writeln

end.
```

Exercises

13.1 A file of results from a marathon race is produced containing, for each race finisher:

race finish position
vest number
race time (hours, minutes, seconds)
surname
initials
sex
age

Define a Pascal **record** to hold the details of one race finisher and write a program that will read a results file, record by record, and print

(a) the total number of men and the total number of women finishing;
(b) details of the oldest male and female runners;
(c) the first three men finishers over 40 years old.

13.2 Write an interactive program to input records to the results file in exercise 13.1. The displayed prompts requesting user input should be as 'friendly' as possible and checks should be made on the input data wherever appropriate.

13.3 Write a program to display a histogram chart with the variables along the *vertical* axis.

(To simplify horizontal scaling you may assume a scale of 0–100 for variable values.)

Further Pascal

The last act is bloody, however charming the rest of the play may be.
Pensées, Blaise Pascal

In attempting to introduce the reader to the fundamentals of computer programming it has been necessary in some cases to omit exhaustive descriptions of certain Pascal features in order to emphasise general principles. Also, a study of the complete Pascal syntax at the end of the book reveals a handful of constructions that have not been mentioned at all. In fact, the volume of material omitted is small, but this is not meant to imply that the extra facilities are never important. The following brief notes are included to give some idea of what you have missed!

14.1 Additional data types

A programmer may define completely new types in Pascal (called 'user-defined types') containing elements that are made up in much the same way as suggested in figure 2.3. Such types are often useful when a variable may be given one of only a limited few values within a program. For example, in a syntax analysis program for English, a variable could be defined to be of type 'partofspeech', say, and set to 'noun', 'adjective', etc. to mark the current part of speech being analysed. One of the most important side-effects of using this facility is the improvement in program readability which ensues.

Although the very useful idea of a constant set (for example, ['A' . . 'Z']) was introduced in chapter 10, Pascal also allows the programmer to define 'set types' which consist of sets of other types. Basic set operations (for example, union, intersection) may then be performed on variables of these types.

173

14.2   Records and pointers

The notion of a special 'pointer' type is perhaps the most important omission from this book. Basically, a variable may be defined as being a 'pointer' to an object of another type and it becomes, effectively, a reference to that other object. Pointers are used almost exclusively as references to records in complex data structures. In its simplest form, a list of records, each containing, for example, details of an item of stock in a warehouse, might be created using pointers rather than, say, an array of records. To do this, each record would contain a 'pointer' to the next record in the list so that the elements of the list could be accessed, in order, by moving down the chain of pointers from one record to the next. List elements could be removed from the list by altering the pointers. A key element in creating data structures of this type is a special standard procedure called *new* which is used to create storage for a new item of data at the end of a pointer, thus allowing the network of records and pointers to expand 'dynamically' (that is, at run-time). This feature is usually used in conjunction with recursion, mentioned below. Another statement, 'with', shown in the syntax diagrams, enables shorthand specification of record fields when pointer mechanisms are used. Also, a reserved word, 'nil' provides a convenient means of assigning a pointer variable to a recognisable 'nothing'.

A rather specialised kind of record construction called a 'variant' record is available to allow records of the same data type to contain data structured in one of several different ways.

14.3   Recursion

Some programming languages, including Pascal, allow a procedure or function to be called from within itself. Such a routine is called a recursive procedure or function and some algorithms are easier to conceive recursively than in terms of repetitive loops, particularly those that manipulate data structures of the kind described above. Perhaps because of a traditional, though today largely indefensible, criticism that it is difficult to use and inefficient to implement, recursion has not achieved its rightful status as a powerful alternative tool in the programmer's armoury.

14.4   Non-text files

If data are to be stored in a file for subsequent reprocessing by a Pascal program those data may be written out to a file of a particular data type and read back in a similar way. Thus, we may have a file of integer or a file of real as well as a text file. A file of records all of one type is a common example of this approach and since all the transformations associated with text file input and output are avoided we would expect the process to be more efficient in both time and storage space.

In some circumstances the data in a file may be 'packed', which means that items in the file are arranged to fit in an optimum way the storage characteristics of a particular computer. Though potentially attractive, this feature does not enhance the portability of programs and data between computers.

14.5   File pointers

In chapter 8 it was mentioned that Pascal provides a means of looking ahead at the next character in an input stream. This character is in fact accessible by using a 'pointer' as described in 14.2, made up of the source file name followed by an 'up-arrow' (↑). Thus, to look at the next character in the standard input file 'input' we may write expressions using 'input↑', as in

```
if input↑ = '.'
then write('Full stop next')
```

Appendix 1: Pascal syntax diagrams

The syntax below describes the Pascal language defined by level zero of the ISO 7185 specification.

Asterisks mark branches in the syntax that have not been explored in the text. Where the word 'identifier' is preceded by another word (for example, 'variable', 'constant') this is for explanatory purposes only and the syntax is identical to that of 'identifier' itself.

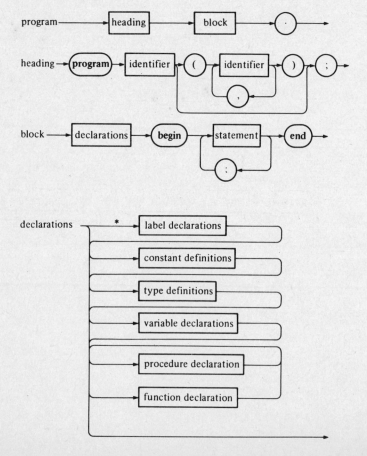

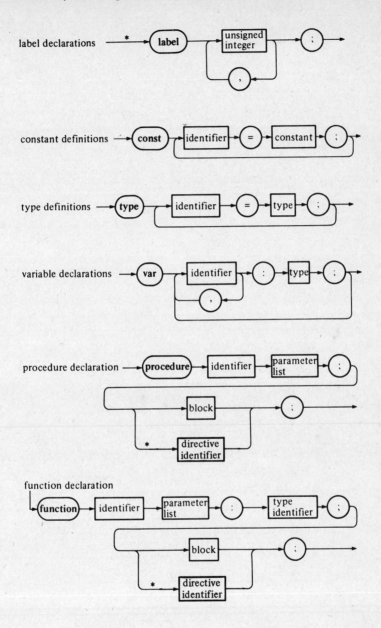

parameter list

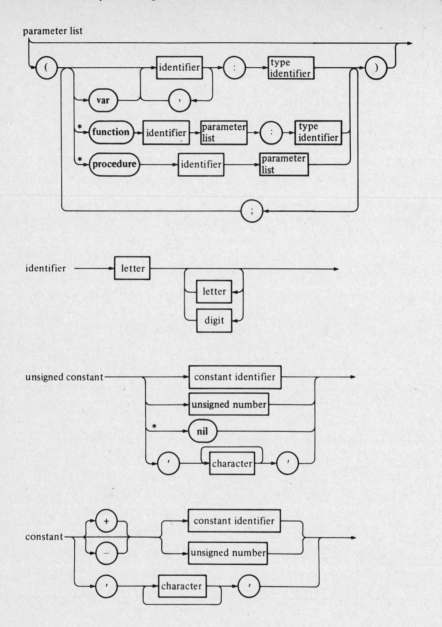

identifier

unsigned constant

constant

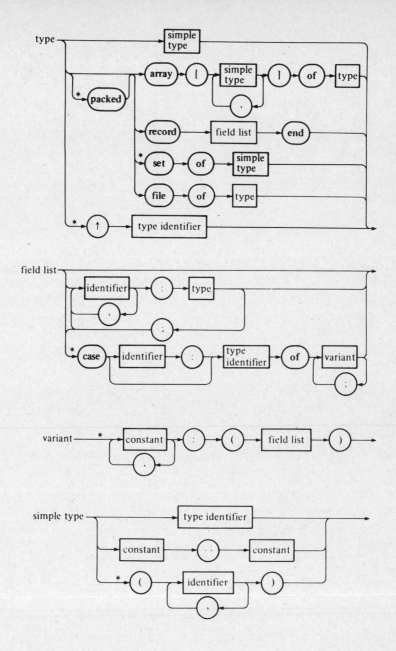

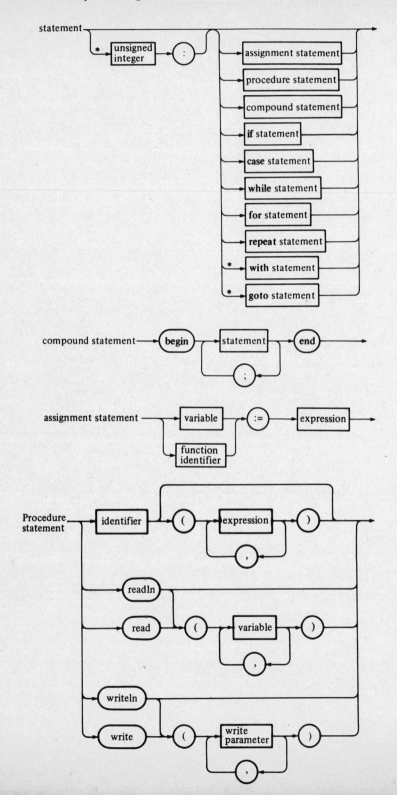

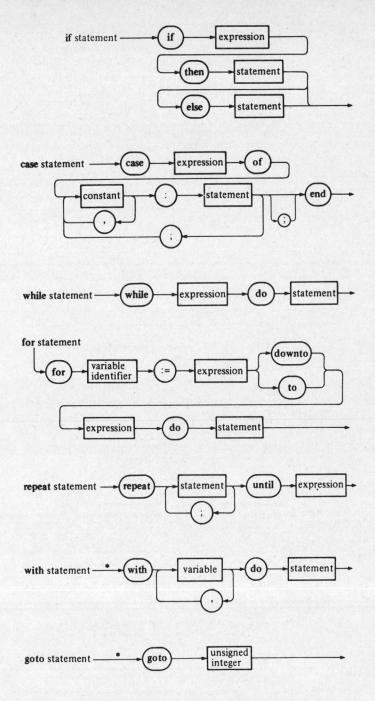

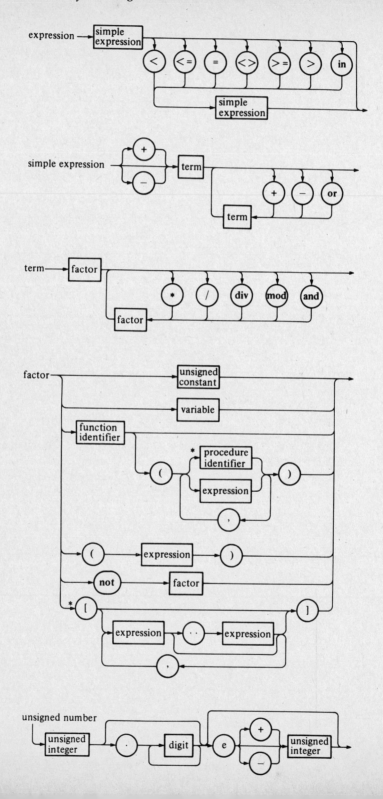

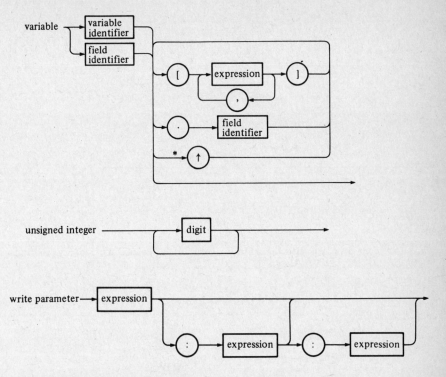

'letter' is upper- or lower-case A to Z

'digit' is 0 to 9

'character' is any member of the character set noting, however, that the single prime
(') must be written twice (").

Appendix 2: Reserved words

and	nil
array	not
begin	of
case	or
const	packed
div	procedure
do	program
downto	record
else	repeat
end	set
file	then
for	to
function	type
goto	until
if	var
in	while
label	with
mod	

Appendix 3: Standard functions

Function	Action	Type of parameters and result
abs(x)	absolute value of x	x is real or integer;
sqr(x)	square of x	result is same type as x
sqrt(x)	square root of x	
sin(x)	sine of x	
cos(x)	cosine of x	x may be integer or real;
exp(x)	e to the power x	result is real
ln(x)	log (base e) of x	
arctan(x)	inverse tangent of x	
eof(x)	indicates end of file x (refers to file 'input' if (x) is omitted)	x is type file; result is Boolean
eoln(x)	indicates end of line in file x (refers to file 'input' if (x) omitted)	x is type text; result is Boolean
odd(x)	'true' if x is odd, 'false' otherwise	x is integer; result is Boolean
trunc(x)	integral part of x $= \text{greatest integer} <= x, x >= 0$ $= \text{least integer} >= x, x < 0$	x is real; result is integer
round(x)	nearest integer to x $= \text{trunc } (x+0.5), x >= 0$ $= \text{trunc } (x-0.5), x < 0$	
ord(x)	the ordinal number of x	x is type char, Boolean or other ordinal;† result is integer
chr(x)	the character whose ordinal number is x	x is integer; result is char
pred(x)	the predecessor of x†	x is ordinal; result is
succ(x)	the successor of x†	same type as x

† Denotes features not explained in detail in this book

Answers to selected exercises from Part 1

2.1 (a) bigcat; puma (b) primenumber; 17 (c) evenones; 1010
2.2 (a) integer (or real) (b) integer (c) real (d) Boolean (e) char
5.1 (a) illegal (hyphen not allowed) (b) legal (c) legal
5.2 oddherd consists of one bull followed by one or more cows
5.3

5.4 (a) $(2*x+y)/3$ (b) sqrt($p/2-q$) (c) $(a+2)*(b-3)$
5.5 (a) double $= 2*$single
   (b) (watertemp $> = 0$) **and** (watertemp $< = 100$)
   (c) (ch $< > $ 'A') **and** (ch $< > $ 'E') **and** (ch $< > $ 'I') **and**
       (ch $< > $ 'O') **and** (ch $< > $ 'U') **and** (ch $< > $ 'a')...etc.
   (d) m **mod** $2 = 0$
5.6 **var** intotal,vatrate:real;
       innumber:integer;
       goodsent:Boolean;
       factory:char;
6.2 **if** a $< > $ b
   then begin
         temp:$=$ a; a:$=$ b; b:$=$ temp
       end
6.3 (a) **case** dig **of**
         0:write('zero');
         1:write('one');
         2:write('two');

```
       · · ·
       · · ·
      9: write('nine')
   end
(b) if (a < b) and (a < c)
      then write('a')
      else if b < c
              then write('b')
              else write('c')
(c) if not ((symbol > = 'A') and (symbol < = 'Z'))
      then write('non-alphabetic')
      else if (symbol = 'A') or (symbol = 'E') or (symbol = 'I')
      or (symbol = 'O') or (symbol = 'U') or (symbol = 'a')
      {...etc. see also chapter 10.6}
              then write('vowel')
              else write('consonant')
```

6.4 **program** larno(input,output);
    var nextnum,largest:real;
      count:integer;
    begin
      read(largest);
      for count:= 2 **to** 20 **do**
        begin
          read(nextnum);
          if nextnum > largest
            then largest:= nextnum
        end;
      write(largest)
    end.

6.5 **program** wheels(input,output);
    var noofwheels:integer;
    begin
      read(noofwheels);
      case noofwheels **of**
        1: write('monocycle');
        2: write('bicycle');
        3: write('tricycle');
        4: write('car')
      end
    end.

6.6 (a) sum:= 0; **for** i:= 1 **to** n **do** sum:= sum+i {or use formulae}
   (b) sum:= 0; **for** i:= 1 **to** n **do** sum:= sum+2∗i

6.7 **program** bandit(input,output);
   var reel1,reel2,reel3:char;
   begin
     write('Enter reel values:');
     if reel1 < > reel2
      then write (' no payout')
      else if reel2 = reel3
       then write(' pay 20p')
       else write(' pay 10p')
   end.

7.2 **program** ctspaces(input,output);
   var spaces:integer;
   procedure countsp(**var** spcount:integer);
   var nextch:char;
   begin
     spcount:= 0;
     while not eoln **do**
      begin
       read(nextch);
       if nextch = ' '
        then spcount:= spcount+1
      end
   end;
   begin {main program}
     countsp(spaces);
     write(spaces, ' spaces found')
   end.

7.3 **procedure** convertgrades (gradeletter,gradequalifier:char;
                      var mark:integer);
   begin
     case gradeletter **of**
      'A':mark:= 1;
      'B':**if** gradequalifier = '+'
        then mark:= 2
        else mark:= 3;
      'C':mark:= 4;
      'D':mark:= 5;
      'E':mark:= 6
     end;

7.4 **function** multiple(x,y:integer):Boolean;
   begin
      multiple:= x **mod** y = 0
   end;
7.5 **function** time(hours,minutes,seconds:integer):integer;
   begin
      time:= hours*3600+minutes*60+seconds
   end;
8.1 write(day:1,'/',month:1,'/',year:4)
   {nb. ':1' is too small a field width here, forcing the number to be
   output in the minimum number of print positions}
8.2 **repeat**
   read(ch1,ch2); {two 'char's}
   day:= ord(ch1)−ord('0');
   if ch2 < > '/'
      then begin
            day:= day*10+ord(ch2)−ord('0');
            read(ch2) {the '/' separator}
         end;
   read(ch1,ch2);
   month:= ord(ch1)−ord('0');
   if ch2 < > '/'
      then begin
            month:= month*10+ord(ch2)−ord('0');
            read(ch2)
         end;
   read(year);
   if day < > 0
      then writeln(day:1,'−',month:1,'−',year:4)
   until day = 0
8.3 **program** line(output);
   var lineno:integer;
   begin {for a 24 line VDU screen}
      for lineno:= 1 **to** 24 **do**
         writeln('   ':round(1.5*lineno),'*')
   end.
8.4 **program** tab(input,output);
   var number,lolimit,hilimit:integer;
   begin
      write('Enter low and high limits:');

```
        read(lolimit,hilimit);
        writeln('number', '    ':3,'square','    ':5,'cube');
        for number:= lolimit to hilimit do
            writeln(number:5,sqr(number):10,number*sqr(number):11)
    end.
8.5 program sos(output);
    const delay = 2000; {increase for faster CPUs}
          short = 1;      {and adjust bleep durations to suit}
          long = 2;
    var count:integer;
    procedure bleep(time:integer);
    var i:integer;
    begin
        for i:= 1 to time do write(chr(7));
        for i:= 1 to delay*time do {do nothing, as a delay}
    end;
    begin {main program}
        for count:= 1 to 3 do bleep(short);
        for count:= 1 to 3 do bleep(long);
        for count:= 1 to 3 do bleep(short)
    end.
```

Index